Geospatial Approaches Modeling for Environmental Water Resources, land use, and Forest Sustainability

ISBN: 9798385761821
Imprint: Independently published
COPYRIGHT C SHAHINAZ EL RAMLY
ESSDS
NO COPY OR DEFORM IS LICENSED

Geospatial Approaches Modeling for Environmental Water Resources, land use, and Forest Sustainability

Geospatial Approaches Modeling for Environmental Water Resources, land use, and Forest Sustainability

- **OVERVIEW OF ENVIRONMENTAL AND WATER RESOURCES**

WATER QUANTUM IN THE WORLD
How much water is there in the world?
What are the resources for water?
On an international scale a little, a little over two-thirds of the water on Earth is frozen glacier and polar ice caps, making up the remaining 3% of the planet's water, which is fresh water. With only a small position present above ground or in the air, the remaining 3% of the planet's water, which is fresh water. With only a small portion present above ground or in the air, the reaming 3% of the planet's water, which is fresh water. Width only a small portion present above grounds in the air, the remaining unfrozen fresh water is mostly found as ground water.

MANAGING OF WATER RESOURCES
What does the term "water resources" mean?
Agriculture, industrial, household, recreational, and environmental activities all make use of water resources. Most applications call for fresh water. However, just 3% of the water on earth is fresh water, with majority (around 97%) being salt water.

WHAT FIVE PLACES ON EARTH HAVE WATER?
Water is (nearly) present practically every where on Earth, including above it in the atmosphere and clouds, below it in the top few miles of the ground, and on its surface in rivers, oceans, ice, plants, and living things.

GENERAL DISTRIBUTION OF WATER RESOURCES
What is the global distribution of Water Resources?
The Oceans contain over 96-5 percent of the planet's total water, covering about 71 percent of its surface. Water also resides in the ground as soil moisture and in aquifers, in the air as water vapor, in rivers, lakes, ice caps, and glaciers, as well as inside of you and your dog.

SEVEN PRINCIPLES OF WATER RESOURCES
What are the seven principal of water sources?
Rain, Ground Water, Ice, Rivers, Lakes, Streams and Natural Reservoirs are the principal sources of water. We obtain water from these sources for daily use.

FOUR SORTS OF WATER RESOURCES
Which four sorts of Water Resources are there?
Natural freshwater resources include ground water, surface water, underground rain fall, and frozen water.

WHAT ROLE DO WATER RESOURCES PLAY
To sustain a sufficient food supply and a productive environment, for all living things, water and water resources are crucial Global Fresh water demand has been rising quickly as human populations and economics expand.

THE REASON WATER IS A PRECIOUS RESOURCE
Why is water a precious resource?
The demands of our environment, our collective agriculture needs, and our personal health, depend on having access to clean water. It serves as the basis for all life and is crucial for sanitation, human rights, urbanization,

ISBN: 9798385761821
Imprint: Independently published
COPYRIGHT C EL RAMLY

Geospatial Approaches Modeling for Environmental Water Resources, land use, and Forest Sustainability

sustainability, and economic development, among other things.

THE ONE PRIMER WATER RESOURCE

What is the one primary water source?

Rainwater is the only natural source of water. It is common for water in lakes, rivers, seas, and ocean and evaporate. The contaminants are evaporated during the elimination process. Rainwater is nearly pure when it hits the earth's surface.

THE NUMBER OF DIFFERENT KINDS OF WATER RESOURCES

What different kinds of water sources are there?

Water comes from two main sources: surface water and ground water. Surface Water, Ground Water and collected Rainwater are the main sources of water used for drinking, Washing, Cooking, Farming, and other industrial application.

THE BEST WATER RESOURCES

What are the best water resources?

Water containing food cucumber. Cucumber has only 8 calories per serving due to its 95% water content. One cup of raw, sliced tomatoes provides 170.14 g of water, making tomatoes an excellent source of water.

Apples, celery, lettuce, watermelon, peaches, water cress and more.

ISBN: 9798385761821
Imprint: Independently published
COPYRIGHT C EL RAMLY

Geospatial Approaches Modeling for Environmental Water Resources, land use, and Forest Sustainability

AUTHOR IMAGE – SHAHINAZ EL RAMLY

ISBN: 9798385761821
Imprint: Independently published
COPYRIGHT C EL RAMLY

Geospatial Approaches Modeling for Environmental Water Resources, land use, and Forest Sustainability

Geospatial Approaches Modeling for Environmental Water Resources, land use, and Forest Sustainability

ISBN: 9798373523271
Imprint: Independently published
COPYRIGHT C SHAHINAZ EL RAMLY
ESSDS
NO COPY OR DEFORM IS LICENSED

CONTENT

PART I: ENVIRONMENT
I. ENVIRONMENTAL AND WATER CHALLENGES FROM MANY ANGLES
II. EARLY CIVILIZATION AQUATIC SETTIING
III. THE WATER H20 CYCLE
IV. WATER OF HIGH QUALITY
V. SIMPLE WTER SHEDS

PART II: WATER RESOURCES
I. UNDERGROUND WATER
II. PONDS AND LAKES
III. STREAMS AND RIVERS
IV. DAMS AND RESEVOIRS IN WET LAND
V. TREATMENT OF WASTEWATER AND DRINKING WATER
ANNEX: REMOTE SENSING

PART III: LAND USE
I. COMMON USES OF LAND
II. IMPORTANCE OF LAND USE
III. TYPES OF LAND
IV. LAND USE CATEGORY
V. FOUR FACTORS OF LAND USE
VI. ELEMENTS OF LAND PLANNING

PART IV: FOREST SUSTAIBABIITY
I. TOWARDS FOREST SUSTAINABILITY
II. THE WICKED PROBLEM OF FOREST POLICY
A MULTI DISCIPLINARY APPROACH FOREST LANDSCAPE
III. MINI FOREST REVOLUTION
IV. GHOST FOREST: RADICALS AND REAL ESTATE
V. FOREST MANAGEMENT AND PLANNING

PART V PROMULGATIONS AND LAWS
I. LAW OF WATER ALLOCATION
II. LAW ENHANCED BY FEDERAL STATE REGIONALLY
III. LOCAL WATER MANAGEMENT
IV. CONFLICT OVER WATER, HS SOLUTION, AND OUR FUTURE
EPILOGUE
INDEX
ADDENDUM: SOUTH AFRICA

ISBN: 9798385761821
Imprint: Independently published
COPYRIGHT C EL RAMLY

Geospatial Approaches Modeling for Environmental Water Resources, land use, and Forest Sustainability

THANKS TO GOD ALL MIGHTY SOVERIEGN OF DOOMS DAY AND THE UIVERSE YOU DO WE ALONE WE WORSHIP AND YOU DO WE ALONE RESORT FOR HELP GUIDE US TO THE STRAIGHT PATH THE PATH OF THOSE WHOM YOUHAVE GIFTED NOR THE ENWRATHED OR WHO WENT ASTRAY.

TO MY DEAREST MUM FAWZYA WHO NEVER WEANED OR COMPLAINED
& MY DEAREST DAD WHO IS A SAGE AND MY LOVELY SISTERS AND NEPHEWS AND NIECE

TO THE WORLD

WITH ♥ and Dedication

ISBN: 9798385761821
Imprint: Independently published
COPYRIGHT C EL RAMLY

Geospatial Approaches Modeling for Environmental Water Resources, land use, and Forest Sustainability

ABOUT THE AUTHOR

Shahinaz El Ramly is Edupreneurship online at ESSDS, Shahinaz read Freshmen when she was 17 years old. Egypt 1993-2022. The inspiration of this book comes from experience as an admin professional career in the field of Water "Judo Water Treatment, Medical Field in operation, qualification, and Calibration. Accounting field in financial statements and auditing and her know how about block chains, her final Job as Administration Manager in BCEOM, DCE, a field of Agronomy, Forestry, Remote sensing, etc. in which she had deep acumen about fossils, reservoirs science, drilling and drains.

Shahinaz is certified by distinction in:

i. e-Learning Ecologies: Innovative Approaches to Teaching and Learning for the Digital Age -
From University of Illinois at Urbana-Champaign

ii.
Innovative Finance: Hacking finance to change the world
From University of Cape Town

iii.
Making Architecture- OFFERED BY MULTIPLE PARTNERS

iv.
Agile Leadership: Introduction to Change
From University of Colorado System

v.
English for Science, Technology, Engineering, and Mathematics

> Great Work! You have passed all requirements and can view your course certificate now.
> From University of Pennsylvania

Vi

Technical Support Fundamentals

Great Work! You have passed all requirements.
From Google

ISBN: 9798385761821
Imprint: Independently published
COPYRIGHT C EL RAMLY

Geospatial Approaches Modeling for Environmental Water Resources, land use, and Forest Sustainability

PART I: SECTION I: ENVIRONMENTAL AND WATER CHALLENGES FROM MANY ANGLES

What environmental issues are connected to the availability of water?
In addition to rain fall, temperature, evaporation rates, soil quality, vegetation type, and water run-off are other significant elements that affect water availability.

Furthermore, there are currently significant challenges in distributing freshwater resources properly among and between nations.

Water Crisis's primary causes water contamination to inadequate sanitation and a lack of waste treatment facilities, the majority of water resources in rural regions are extremely filthy.

Over drafting ground water, excessive and proper use of water, disease climatic change, poor management, human settlement, and corruption.

What are the top 5 dangers to the availability of water?
There are five. dangers to the water that supports our agriculture.
- Adrification and dry conditions.
- Improper ground water management.
- A saltwater invasion.
- Pollution.

LAND DEGREDATION: REMEDIES

What are the reasons? for the problem with water?
Water scarcity primary causes:
- Global warming.
- Natural disasters including floods and droughts increased consumption by people.
- Excessive water uses and waste.
- A gross in freshwater demand globally.
- Overuse of aquifers and sluggish recharging as a result.

What are three water challenges that the world is currently facing?
The decade is about stepping up efforts to address issue to water, such as inadequate access to clean water and sanitary facilities. Water resources and increased danger of drought and floods.

What elements have an impact on the Water Environment?
The quality of the water is influenced by many things:
- Sedimentation
- Run off
- Erosion
- Oxygen in solution.
- PH. Is Temperature.
- Organic compounds in decay Pesticides.

ISBN: 9798385761821
Imprint: Independently published
COPYRIGHT C EL RAMLY

Geospatial Approaches Modeling for Environmental Water Resources, land use, and Forest Sustainability

What elements have an impact on the Water Environment?
How can we overcome the problems of water?
There are several strategies to conserve water and avoid water shortages: environmental water management. As efficient and effective use of water are essential elements of sustainable water management improving water infrastructure must be a top concern. Reclaimed water, better sewage treatment and pollution control, awareness and education.

What poses the greatest risk to water?
- Water quality threats.
- Pollutants from a single point.
- Polluting-nonpoint sources.
- Run off from agriculture.
- The water that flows into the waster sheds combine with pesticides, herbicides, fungicides, and other chemical that farmers employ on their crops or animals.
- Urbanization, urban runoff, and septic waste.

What consequences do environmental issues have?
Food and Water insecurity, respiratory illness and diseases, mental discomfort and emotional health issues, family division, loss of social networks, property damage, unemployment, interruption of income, and asset depletion are common repercussions, social justice concerns also to pertain to environmental change.

What are the six environmental factors?
Climate-related variables are referred to by the term LOWERN. Latitude It is based on the amount of sunshine and the region that it affects, as well as how close or far it is from the equator.
Ocean currents, wind and air currents elevation, relief, and proximity to water.

What are the difficulties in managing water?
India, some of the main issues with managing water for agriculture and other requirements include floods, water logging, social erosion, drought, salty ground water, etc.

What are some fun Aquatic challenges?
Why it is crucial to safeguard the aquatic environment?
Life need water to exist. For drinking and sanitation, for our food, cattle, and industry as well as for the development and maintenance of the ecosystems that support all life, clean fresh water is a must.

What impact does a scarcity of water have on the environment?
In adequate water availability can have a negative impact on the ability of soils to support crops, increase dust production, owing to dryness, cause erosion, and raise the risk of wildfires due to the dry environment fish, animals and plant life can be impacted by a shortage of water and by the soil's decreased capacity to support crops.

What causes Water Contamination and What harm does it do to the environment?
Though streams and rivers, pollutants and pesticides, nutrients and heavy metals are transported from farms,

ISBN: 9798385761821
Imprint: Independently published
COPYRIGHT C EL RAMLY

Geospatial Approaches Modeling for Environmental Water Resources, land use, and Forest Sustainability

industries and cities into our bays and estuaries, where they are transported out to sea. While this is happening marine trash, particularly plastic, is carried in by wind or washes up through storm drains and sewers.

How does the changing Climate affect water availability?

Millions of people rely on freshwater resources, but seal levels rise, they are becoming increasingly saline.

Why is Egypt's being lack of a problem?
The Nile River, Egypt's primary source of water, has diminished because of prolonged droughts and an increasingly hot and arid climate, a problem that affect many waters supplies across the world.

The main Calamity of Egypt is deprived of the inundation.

What are the top three dangers to the oceans?
Here are the top five problems that our oceans are currently facing, along with solutions.
Global warming, Ocean health is arguably most at risk from climate change, followed by plastic pollution, sustainable sea food, marine protected areas, and fisheries subsidiaries.

ISBN: 9798385761821
Imprint: Independently published
COPYRIGHT C EL RAMLY

Geospatial Approaches Modeling for Environmental Water Resources, land use, and Forest Sustainability

SECTION II. EARLY CIVILIZATION AQUATIC SETTING

Why did early societies center themselves around water?
In early, developing civilizations, water served three basic functions: it was necessary for drinking, it had to be avoided as a natural hazard like a flood, and it provided a conductive environment for fishing and hunting.

What were the top three reasons, why civilization was founded close to water sources?
The locals can depend on a river to provide them with water for drinking and cultivation. Fishing, fertile soil from yearly flooding, and accessibility of travel are further advantages. All the earliest major civilizations, including those in Mesopotamia and Ancient Egypt, developed in river valleys.

What were the first four rivers in Human History?
The Tigers and Euphrates in Mesopotamia (modern Iraq), the River Nile in Egypt, and the yellow and blue rivers in China are just a few of the major rivers where the earlies civilizations originally emerged 5000 years ago.

How was water preserved in prehistoric societies?
Water may have been transported in prehistoric times via plant shells like coconuts, animal horns, or the stretched baskets used to transport water were later sealed with day or mind. In 5000 BC, people in antiquity started carrying water in ceramic.

How did early societies transfer water?
Aqueducts, or canals, have been constructed by engineers to transport water, sometimes over long distance. Aqueducts were just created in the high-tech modern day; the ancient Romans used them to transport water from the high lands above Rome, Italy, to the city.

Why did early civilizations to settle close to rivers?
A portion of the population was liberated from the reliance on food gathering and hunting because of the rivers provision of abundant drinking water and fertile soil for the start of food crop production.

Why did early humans' dwell near bodies of water?
Because they required fresh water to survive and cultivate food, early people made their homes near rivers and streams.

What function does water serve in a society?
The quality and quantity of safe drinking and survival water is a direct constraint on civilization. Additionally, they are restricted indirectly by how water affects agriculture, industry, transportation, and energy.

What did ancient Humans Value water so highly?
Villages, cities, and finally states were all built through sedentary agriculture life and were all heavily reliant on water. Humans and water now have a whole unique relationship as a result. The sedentary farmers were exposed to a very high health risk from pathogens spread by polluted water.

Why do successful civilizations need water systems?
Most historical civilizations developed around big rivers, particularly when those rivers flowed into the sea. Tribes

ISBN: 9798385761821
Imprint: Independently published
COPYRIGHT C EL RAMLY

Geospatial Approaches Modeling for Environmental Water Resources, land use, and Forest Sustainability

that were far from rivers were typically forced to remain nomadic. Rivers gives civilizations a source of fresh, healthy water that they may use for themselves, their livestock, and their crops.

Why did the first societies rely on river flooding?
Because rivers water ways offered locations for hunting and fishing civilizations grew up around them. The surrounding area also became productive because of the rivers flooding. They could now support farming thanks to this.

What impact has water had on human Civilization?
Ancient Civilization built water mills to process wheat, perfected drainage and built canals, aqueducts, and pipes to transport water. They invented aquifer water drainage by constructing canals as well as water display buildings for aesthetic purposes.

Why were early Communities located near rivers?
Because there was lots of water and fertile land near the river valleys, settlements flourished there.

Why did the first four Civilizations emerge around a river?
The early Civilizations emerged in a large river valley, where flood plains held fertile from land and rivers offered irrigation and transportation.

What exactly are the four river Civilizations?
Historically, all the first great Civilizations arose along river valleys. Historians consider the four RVC to be the world's first great Civilizations. The Tigris – Euphrates River, the Nile River Valley, the Indus River Valley, and the Huang- He River Valley are the names of these rivers.

What were the four Civilizations, and what rivers were located nearby?
The First Civilizations
The most noteworthy examples are the Ancient Egyptians, who were based on the Nile, the Mesopotamians in the fertile Crescent on the Tigris, Euphrates rivers, the Ancient Chinese on the Yellow River, and the Ancient Indians on the Indus.

How many river Civilizations exist?
Valley of the Four Rivers
Civilizations and Locations in the Four River Valley. In Mesopotamia, the major four river valley Civilizations.

Which River Valley Civilization was the most prosperous?
In-modern-day India and Pakistan, a massive ancient Civilization evolved in the Indus River Valley. For a time, around 2500 BCE, it was one of the world's greatest Civilizations.

How numerous were the early river civilizations?
Geography what rivers aided in the survival of the four river valley civilizations? Irrigation systems, for example, required leadership and laws – the beginnings of organized government. Priests Controlled the first Government in some countries.

ISBN: 9798385761821
Imprint: Independently published
COPYRIGHT C EL RAMLY

Geospatial Approaches Modeling for Environmental Water Resources, land use, and Forest Sustainability

Why was Egypt dubbed a river Civilization?
The Nile provided food and suppliers, agriculture land, transportation, and was critical in delivering materials for building projects and other large–scale undertakings in Egypt. It was a vital lifetime that practically breathed life into the barren.

Which culture is referred to as the "Land between Rivers"?
Civilizations of Mesopotamia
Mesopotamian civilizations flourished between the Euphrates and Tigris rivers. "Meso" means between and "Postamus" means "river" in Greek. As a result, the civilization is known as Mesopotamian Civilization.

Did the pyramids have water?
When the Nile flooded in the summer, massive dikes were constructed to drain water from the river and channel it to the pyramid via an artificial canal system, establishing an internal port that allowed boasts to dock very near to work site – just a few hundred meters away from the building pyramid.

Egypt used to be an Ocean, right?
The fossilized remnants are aiding in the discovery of how much of Egypt was once covered by a massive ancient ocean 50 million years ago.

Did the Pyramids have water?
When the Nile flooded in the summer, massive dykes were constructed to drain water from the river and channel it to the pyramid via an artificial canal system, establishing an inland port that allowed boats to dock very near.

What impact has water had on human Civilization?
Ancient Civilization built water mills to process wheat, perfected drainage and built canals, aqueducts, and pipes to transport water drainage by constructing aquifer water drainage by constructing Canals, as well as water display buildings.

What was the main source of water in Egyptian Civilization?
The Nile, which runs 4, 160 miles north from east-central Africa to the Mediterranean, provided ancient Egypt with excellent soil and water for irrigation, as well as a way of delivering building materials. Its life-giving rivers allowed cities to develop amid a desert.

Where did the Iron Age acquire its water?
The Warren Shaft Crammed after Captain C. Warren, who uncovered it in the nineteenth century was an older Iron Age system that provided free access to water via network of underground tunnels a shaft.

Was Water present during the stone Age?
Water is available from streams, rivers, and springs, of course. Settlements were typically located near fresh water sources. Water from these sources would have been clean prior to the industrialization of the planet, however people could have cooked it as well.

Did the ancients filter their water?
As early as 1, 500 BC, the Ancient Egyptians developed the water cleaning procedure known as Coagulation.

ISBN: 9798385761821
Imprint: Independently published
COPYRIGHT C EL RAMLY

Geospatial Approaches Modeling for Environmental Water Resources, land use, and Forest Sustainability

Coagulation is now defined as the process of neutralizing changes and producing a gelatinous mass to capture particles, resulting in a mass large enough to settle or be caught in the filter.

In ancient Egypt, how was water transported?
The Shadouf was used by ancient Egyptians to send water to regions far from the Nile's banks.

Did irrigation systems exist in ancient Egypt?
The Egyptians invented and used a method of water management known as basin irrigation. The approach enabled them to manage the river's rise and fall to best fit their agricultural demands.

In Egypt, how is water used?
Approximately 85% of Egypt's water resources are used for agricultural irrigation systems, which have substantial water loses and low efficiency.

How did the ancient Greeks move water?
Because of the rapid expansion in urban population in ancient Greece, via aqueducts, store water in citizens and dams, and distribute it to the people via networks. The treated wastewater, together with rainwater, was transported away via sewers.

How does Egypt obtain clean Water?
The Nile River in Egypt's primary supply of fresh water. Every year, the river provides 56.8 billion m^3 Of fresh water, accounting for 97% of Egypt's renewable water resources. Egypt's average annual rain fall's is predicted to be 18 mm (1.8) billion m^3.

Where did ancient Rome acquire its Water?
The Roman aqueducts provided fresh, clean water baths, fountains, and ordinary folk's drinking waver.

Where did Arabs acquire their water?
Saudi Arabia is largely reliant on two sources of water: ground water and water derived from desalination plants that remove salt from sea water. Ground water is derived from beneath the earth's crust, where there is a large layer of water that is obtained through wells, bore wells, and other means.

Where did the first Human find Water?
The study of rocks and soil from ancient lakes, as well as the bones of creatures like as hippopotamus or hippos, suggest that water was present.

Where did Israel obtain its water?
To meet the rising demand, Israel's national water utility, Mekorot, has begun building the National water from Northern Lake Kinneret (sea of Galilee) and transmit it to central and southern Israel from regional water projects.

Where did Medieval Folks get their drinking water?
Fresh water sources were used to build medieval villages and towns. This could from a spring or, in many cases, from wells.

ISBN: 9798385761821
Imprint: Independently published
COPYRIGHT C EL RAMLY

Geospatial Approaches Modeling for Environmental Water Resources, land use, and Forest Sustainability

Was Saudi Arabia ever and Ocean?

Saudi Arabia was under water during the Early Cretaceous period, according to the Ancient Earth Globe, which was launched by paleontologist Ian Webster, the earth had no polar ice caps at the time, therefore water levels were much greater than they are today.

Was Saudi Arabia a Tropical Rain Forest?

Riyadh: According to experts, big findings in various sections of Saudi Arabia are likely to change the world's perspective of the Gulf ancient history.

ISBN: 9798385761821
Imprint: Independently published
COPYRIGHT C EL RAMLY

Geospatial Approaches Modeling for Environmental Water Resources, land use, and Forest Sustainability

SECTION III: THE WATER H₂O CYCLE

The Water Cycle depicts the ongoing circulation of water within the Earth's atmosphere's atmosphere. It's a complicated system with numerous processes. Liquid water evaporates into water vapor, condenses into clouds, and falls back to earth on rain and snow.

THE FOUR STAGES OF WATER CYCLE
So how we comprehend this mysterious process known as the Water Cycle?
The Water Cycle is divided into four stages: Evaporation, Conventions, Precipitation, and Collection.
Evaporation occurs when the sun heats water in rivers, lakes, or the Ocean, converting it to vapor or steam.

THE SEVEN STAGES OF THE WATER CYCLE
It can be investigated by beginning with Evaporation, Condensation, Precipitation, Interception, Infiltration, per collection, Transpiration, Run Off, or Storage.

FIVE PHASES OF WATER CYCLE
What are the five phases of the Water Cycle?
Many systems interact to keep the Earth's water circulating in a cycle. The hydrologic cycle involves five processes; Condensation, Precipitation, Infiltration, Run, and Evapotranspiration.

THE THREE DISTINCTION STAGES OF THE WATER CYCLE
Evaporation in the first of three major processes in the hydrologic Cycle: Condensation, Run off from the surface.

SIGNIFICANCE OF THE WATER CYCLE
The hydrologic cycle is critical since it is the means by which water reaches plants, animals, and us? Aside from providing water for people, animals, and us!
Aside from providing water for people, animals, and plants, it also transports nutrients, diseases, and sediments, into and out of aquatic habitats.

PHASE OF WATER CYCLE VARIANCE
The total number of water particles remains constant when water changes states in water cycle. Melting, sublimation, evaporation, freeing, condensation, and deposition and examples of states shifts. All states change the flow of Energy.

THE QUANTUM STATES OF WATER CYCLE
The water cycle has four major stages. Evaporation, Condensation, Precipitation and Collecting are the four processes.

DIFFERENT PHASES OF WATER
Water exists in three different stages: solid, liquid and gas. Water molecules link with hydrogen atoms of surrounding water molecules that are arranged in a specific order. The molecules move but do not circulate.

ISBN: 9798385761821
Imprint: Independently published
COPYRIGHT C EL RAMLY

Geospatial Approaches Modeling for Environmental Water Resources, land use, and Forest Sustainability

WATER CYCLE REPRESENTED BY DIAGRAM

The Water Cycle is defined as a natural process of recycling water in the atmosphere on a continuous basis. The hydrological cycle is also known as the hydrologic cycle. Water changes states of matter during the water cycle between the earth and the atmosphere: solid, liquid and gas.

ISBN: 9798385761821
Imprint: Independently published
COPYRIGHT C EL RAMLY

Geospatial Approaches Modeling for Environmental Water Resources, land use, and Forest Sustainability

SECTION IV: WATER OF THE HIGH QUALITY

THE BEST DRINKING WATER
The following countries are regarded to have the cleanest drinking water in the world:
DENMARK: Denmark's tape water is superior to bottled water. ICELAND… GREEN LAND… FINLAND… COLOMBIA… SINGAPHORE---- NEWZELAND-----SWEDEN.

THE SIGNINFICANCE OF GOOD WATER
The value of good water cannot be overstated. One of the most significant risk factors for the spread of infectious diseases such as polio, typhoid, cholera, dysentery, hepatitis, and diarrhea, is a lock of access to clean and safe water.

TYPES OF WATER QUALITY
Water quality parameters are classified into three types: Physical, Chemical, and Biological.

THE BEST WATER QUALITY
Finland and Scandinavia
When you add them all up, it's evidence that this region of the world has some of the cleanest and safest water coming from taps. Finland filters its naturally clean water numerous times before it reaches the tap just for good measure.

PUREST COUNTRIES WATER ARE:
These are the countries on the world with the cleanest drinking water:
Greece, Iceland, Ireland, Italia.
THE COUNTRY OF THE NETHERLANDS, NORWAY, SWITZERLAND, AND UNITED KINGDOM.

SAFE WATER
Rainwater contains germs and other pollutants. While rainwater is useful for many things, it is not as pure as you may imagine, thus you should not drink it.

GREATEST WATER
In all Arabic and Islamic countries, Zamzam water is the most favored potable water and is regarded superior to other drinking water sources. The water well in Zamzam is sterile and free of bacteria and fungi.

ISBN: 9798385761821
Imprint: Independently published
COPYRIGHT C EL RAMLY

Geospatial Approaches Modeling for Environmental Water Resources, land use, and Forest Sustainability

SECTOPM V: SIMPLE WATER SHEDS

WATER SHED MEANING
It is a geo graphical area that directs rainwater and snow melt to Creeks, Streams and Rivers, finally Draining to Reservoirs, Bays and the Ocean.

EXCELLENT EXAMPLE OF WATER SHED
A Water Shed is a geographical area that comprises a common network of streams and rivers that all flow into a single bigger body of water, such as a larger, river, a lake, or the ocean.
The Mississippi River Water Shed, for example is massive.

BASIC COMPONENTS OF WATER SHED
A Water Shed is made up of multiple water courses, including the land surrounding them. All of which drain into a single place at a lower elevation. It is made up of two basic components: Water and Land.

SIGNIFICANCE OF THE TERM WATER SHED
Term WATER SHED: -
However, the phrase was originally used to describe a location where water sources drop into a single river formed by a chain of mountains that distributes Water to two different rivers or either side. Water shed came to represent a turning point or dividing line in life because of this.

VARIOUS SOURCE OF WATER SHED
There are many sorts of Water sheds Macro Water Shed (more than 50, 000 Hecht.) (10 000 to 50 000 HECT) Milli Water Shed (1000 to 10 000 HECT), THE MICRO WATER SHED (100 TO 1000 HECT) Miniature Water Shed (1-100 HECT).

WHAT ARE FIVE MAIN WATER SHEDS?
The Great Basin, the St. Basin, the St. Lawrence Basin, the Arctic Basin, the Hudson Bay Basin, and the Great Basin.

REFERENCE TO WATER SHED
When two neighboring rivers meet in geography. One's 'sheds' into another at the meeting place. The phrase has gained currency in the media. Two audiences, adults, and youngsters, merge into one, only adults.

ELEMENTS THAT MAKE UP A WATER SHED
THE CONCEPTUAL UNDERPINING FOR HEALTHY WATER SHED is described in this section. It then goes over each of the six assessment components in depth, including landscape condition, habitat, hydrology, geomorphology, water quality, and biological condition.

GOVERNANCE OF WATER SHEDS
WATER SHEDS management is an endeavor to halt land degradation and a comprehensive procedure for maximizing land productivity. Watershed management entails the rational use of land and water resources for optimum and sustained output while posing the least amount of risk to natural resources.

ISBN: 9798385761821
Imprint: Independently published
COPYRIGHT C EL RAMLY

Geospatial Approaches Modeling for Environmental Water Resources, land use, and Forest Sustainability

PLANTS SAFEGUARD WATER SHED
INCORPORATE native plants or a rain garden into your landscaping.
For one thing, thick roots hold soil in place and prevent erosion. Second, deep roots transport water into the ground. Native plants run off and recharge ground water resources by infiltrating water into the earth.

WATER SHED protecting healthy water sheds can reduce capital expenses for water treatment plants as well as damage to properly and infrastructure caused by flooding, minimizing future costs.

WHO CREATED WATER SHED?
F. Meyer proposed one of the most prevalent waters shed algorithms in the early 1990s, although a few modifications, collectively known as a Priority Flood. Have since been made to this technique, including variants appropriate for data sets including trillions of pixels. The algorithms are applied to grey scale image.

WATER SHED IN GEOGRAPHY
A river Basin also known as a drainage basin, is a region of land drained by a river and its tributaries. The watershed is the margin of the drainage basin. This is the analogous to a skin or basin that collects the water that falls into it.

WATER SHED CAUSE
Watershed dubbed itself "Britain's First Media Centre" when it opened its doors in 1982, hoping to capture and contextualize the revolution in media at the time when satellite TV and Channel 4 were just getting started.

DIFFERENT SORTS OF WATER RESOURCES
Natural Fresh Water sources include surface water, subsurface river flow, ground water, and frozen water.

EXACT HEALTHY WATER SHED
A healthy watershed is one in which natural land cover supports the following processes: dynamic hydrologic processes within their natural range of fluctuation, habitat of sufficient size and connectedness to sustain native aquatic and riparian process.

SIGNIFICANCE OF WATESHED BIODIVERSITY
Watershed gather rainfall and spread run off to support all types of life in the habitats found within them.

WATERSHED NATURAL OR ARTIFICIAL Watershed are natural systems with Which we can collaborate.

EXPLAINING WATERSHED TO A CHILD
A watershed is a system of water where every think comes together. When it rains, for example, you may notice small streams of water running along a roadway gutter or across a packing lot. These run into larger streams, then it puddles or sewage pipes, and sometimes into a real stream of river.

FOOT NOTE
PHILLIPINES: [Employing a technique at clearing by slashing and burning under bush and trees and plowing the ashes under for fertilizer].

ISBN: 9798385761821
Imprint: Independently published
COPYRIGHT C EL RAMLY

Geospatial Approaches Modeling for Environmental Water Resources, land use, and Forest Sustainability

EXACT WATER SHED RULE
The "WATER SHED" Doctrine provide convicts with a constitutional Foundation for re-opening their cases based on new due process protections if publicized before their appeals were exhausted.

HOW DO WATER SHEDS EVOLVE THROUGH OUT TIME?
Change is essential part of the watershed. The significance fluctuations in river and stream flow after short lines, streamlines, stream channels, and stream corridors on a regular basis. Water shed uplands after because of biological succession disease, competition, human activity, and other reasons.

WHERE DOES A WATERSHED STARTS AND WHERE DOES IT END?
A watershed is a land area that drains to a body water, such as river or a lake. In Highlands, water enters the water shed from rain or snow melt. Water flows from the water shed divide at the highest altitudes to the body of water to the lowest point in watershed.

CAUSATION OF WATER SHED DESTRUCTION
Watershed direct cause these include the absence or inadequate maintenance of erosion control measures in upland farms, inappropriate crop rotations, a shorter fallow period in Kaingin agriculture, insufficient or excessive fertilizer use, and irrigation water abuse.

WHAT IS ANOTHER WORD FOR WATER SHED?
The synonym is basin for drainage. Drainage is area is a noun, catchment area. The catchment basin.

WHAT IS THE MOST SERIOUS THREAT TO WATERSHEDS?
- Reports on Watersheds.
- Overall dangers
- Loss of Habitat
- Fragmentation of Habitat.
- Excessive use of water
- Species that are invasive.
- Changes in the climate.
- Flows are being changed.

WHAT EXACTLY IS A CULTURAL WATER SHED?
Through reflection, art, and debate, the cultural water shed activity is intended to bridge and harmonize personal identity and landscape.

EFEECT OF WATER SHED ON ECO SYSTEM
Many ecosystem services are provided by healthy watersheds, including but not limited to nutrients cycling, carbon storage, erosion, sedimentation, control, increased biodiversity, soil formation, water storage, water filtration, flood control, timber, and recreation as well as reduced.

ISBN: 9798385761821
Imprint: Independently published
COPYRIGHT C EL RAMLY

Geospatial Approaches Modeling for Environmental Water Resources, land use, and Forest Sustainability

CLIMATE CHANGE INFLUENCE ON WATER SHED
Climate change affects water sheds by affecting the quantity, quality, timing, and distribution of water. Climate change exacerbates the cumulative effects CUM historical land-uses, water withdrawals, and disturbances in water shed.

FOUR QUALITIES USED TO CATEGORIZE WATER SHED
Basin area, basin length, basins slope, and basin shape are physical characteristics of watersheds that influence turn off and other hydrologic processes.

THE LARGEST WATERSHED OF THE WORLD
THE AMAZON BASIN IS BY FAR THE LARGEST IN THE WORLD, Composing one third of the South American Continent.

ISBN: 9798385761821
Imprint: Independently published
COPYRIGHT C EL RAMLY

Geospatial Approaches Modeling for Environmental Water Resources, land use, and Forest Sustainability

PART II. SECTION I. UNDERGROUND WATER

DAM FOR IRRIGATION
Irrigation Dams and reservoirs are built to retain excess water during water periods, which can then be used to irrigate arid territories. One of the primary advantages of dams and reservoirs in that water flows can be adjusted to meet agricultural needs of various regions throughout the year.

RIVER RESERVOIR
In many people's minds, a reservoir is the same as a lake. A reservoir, on the other hand, is a man-made lake formed when a dam is built over a river. A reservoir is formed when river water backs up behind the dam.

ILLUTRATION OF WATER RESERVOIR
OCEANS, glaciers, freshwater, lakes, rivers, and live beings are examples. These are reservoirs from which we can draw water if we can so desire.

DISTINCTION BETWEEN A DAM AND A RESEVOIR
A dam is built to stop or restrict the flow of water or substrate streams. In contrast, a reservoir is an open-air storage space (often built by masonry or earthwork) where water is gathered to be drawn for usage.

DAMS NECESSARY FOR IRRIGATION
Dams and Canals store and supply for irrigation.

TYPES OF RESEVOIRS
RESEVOIRS CLARIFICATION STORAGE OR CONVERSION RESERVOIRS
- RESERVOIRS FOR FLOOD CONTROL
- RESERVOIRS FOR DISTRIBUTION
- RESEVOIRS THAT PROVIDE MULTIPLE FUCNTIONS

WATER RESERVOIRS
WATER has been dispersed throughout Earth's history between four major reservoirs the ocean, ice sheets and glaciers (the cryosphere), terrestrial, and the atmosphere.

RESEVOIRS WATER
Water has been dispersed throughout Earth's history between four major reservoirs: the Oceans, Ice Sheets, and glaciers (the cryosphere), terrestrial storage, and the atmosphere.

DIFFERENCE BETWEEN DAM AND A RESEVOIR
A dam is built to stop or restrict the flows of water or subsurface streams. In Contrast a Reservoir is an open – air storage space (often build by masonry or earth and work) where water is gathered and stored in sufficient amount to be drawn off for usage.

The major distinction between a river and a reservoir is that one fosters life while the other suppresses it. Rivers are active bodies of flowing water. Their banks support crops as other natural existing plants and greenery.

Geospatial Approaches Modeling for Environmental Water Resources, land use, and Forest Sustainability

KINDS OF DIFFERENT WATER RESEVOIRS
A Dam is built to stop or restrict the flow of water or subsurface streams. In contrast a Reservoir is an open – air storage space (often built by masonry or earth work) where water is gathered and stored in sufficient amount to bd drawn off for usage.

DISTINCTION BETWEEN A RIVER AND RESEVOIR
The major distinction between a river and a reservoir is that one fosters life while the other suppresses it. Rivers are active bodies of flowing water. Their banks support crops as well as other natural existing plants and greenery.

KINDS OF DIFFERENT WATER RESEVOIRS
The major distinction between a river and a reservoir is that one fosters life while the other suppresses it. Rivers are active bodies of flowing water. Their banks support crops as well as other natural existing plants and greenery.

KINDS OF DIFFERENT WATER RESEVOIRS
RESEVOIRS are classified into three type Valley dammed bank side, and service reservoirs. Valley-dammed and bank side reservoirs can be both Natural and Man-made where server reservoirs are wholly man made.

FIVE MAIN RESERVOIRS
Rock, Atmosphere, Oceans, Terrestrial, Biosphere, and Fossil are the five major carbon reservoirs.

SIX WATER RESEVOIRS
Oceans, glaciers, freshwater lakes, rivers, ground water, and live beings are examples. These are reservoirs from which we can draw water if we so desire.

THE DIFFERENT TYPES OF RESEVOIRS
Reservoirs are classified into two types of lake reservoirs and river reservoirs are characterized by the formation of bodies of water with physical qualities that differ greatly from those of incoming water.

BENEFITS OF DAMS AND RESEVOIRS
They can also be used to control the flow of water in rivers. During dry seasons, water can be released from the reservoir to help wildlife and the environment downstream, as well as to provide a resource for human use.

DAMS AND RESEVOIRS KEEP FLOODING AT BAY
ENGINEERS can restrict the flow of a river by constructing dam, which can then be utilized to prevent floods during heavy rains.

THE PRIMARY PROCESSES IN THE TREATMENT OF RESEVOIR WATER TREATMENT PROCEDURES
Coagulation: Coagulation is frequently the initial stage in water treatment. Coagulation is followed by flocculation sedimentation. Sedimentation is one of the processes used to extract solids from water filtration…. Disinfection.

ISBN: 9798385761821
Imprint: Independently published
COPYRIGHT C EL RAMLY

Geospatial Approaches Modeling for Environmental Water Resources, land use, and Forest Sustainability

FOUR EXAMPLES OF NATRUAL RESEVOIRS
Field mice are natural reservoirs for manta viruses and Lassa disease.
Bubonic plague in mar mots, black rats, prairie dogs, chipmunks, and squirrels. Chagas disease is spread by armadillos and opossums. Babesiosis and Rocky Mountains spotted fever tricks.

RESEVOIRS IN PEOPLE'S VIEW ON THE OTHER HAND
Reservoirs: In many people's views, a reservoir is synonymous with a lake reservoir on the other hand, is a man-made lake formed when a dam is built over a river. A reservoir is formed when river water backs up behind the dam.

RESEVOIR NOMENCLATURE
Reservoir is a big residential area located kilometers of central Melbourne and two kilometers north of Preston in 1864, 1909 and 1913 to contain the metro polytan water supply from the Yan Yean Reservoir.

FIVE DRAW BACKS OF DAMS
DAM ADVENTAGES
People are displaced during construction Reservoirs frequently emit a large proportion of greenhouse gases. Frequently destroys local ecosystems. It causes a disruption in the ground table. Water cannot flow to other TO

ROLES OF DAMS AND RESERVOIRS
IN WATER PLANING
DAMS are often built to hold water in a reservoir, which is then used for a variety of purposes, including agriculture and municipal water. Supplies. Reservoir water can also be directed to flow via hydraulic turbines, generating electricity for use in homes and businesses.

RESEVOIRS KEEP THEIR WATER
There are a few ways to accomplish this, so here are some pointers for keeping a clean water reservoir.
Inspect you tank water reservoir clean by inspecting it on a regular basis for damage, leaks, and other system flaws. Make use of tank liners.

BURSTING DAMS
Using sandbags to raise free board and avoid overtopping, riprap to prevent down structure erosion, or geotextile filter clothes combat piping are all examples of emergency intervention measures that can be employed to try to preserve a dam total failure.

WATER TREATMENT METHODS
TOP 7 WATER TREATMENT METHODS Coagulation is also known as flocculation. Coagulation is the addition of liquid aluminum surface oralum, as well as a polymer, to sedimentation: when water and Flocs are treated, they are deposited in sedimentation basins. filtration...disinfection…..sludge....drying… fluoridation…PTL correction.

TWO BASIC STEPS IN TREATING RESEVOR WATER PURIFICATION
DISSOLVED FLOTATION: Water is delivered into a chamber with chemicals added to bind any particles together. Sand filtration: Water runs through fine sand filter beds, trapping any left-over particles.

ISBN: 9798385761821
Imprint: Independently published
COPYRIGHT C EL RAMLY

Geospatial Approaches Modeling for Environmental Water Resources, land use, and Forest Sustainability

MUST CRUCIAL STEP IN THE PURIFICATION OF WATER COGULATION

In the other hand, is a critical fundamental step in the water treatment process because interlaminations many of the particles that make water difficult to disinfect, such as dissolved organic carbon. Because civilization eliminates some of the dissolved chemicals, the amount of chlorine required to disinfect the water is reduced.

Geospatial Approaches Modeling for Environmental Water Resources, land use, and Forest Sustainability

SECTION II PONDS AND LAKES

Ponds and lakes are both inland bodies of fresh water with live organisms. They appear to be extremely similar at first sight-! Both depth and surface area must be evaluated to assist determine the difference. Lakes are often significantly deeper and have a bigger surface area than ponds.

THE MAIN DISTINCTION BETWEEN PONDS AND "LAKES" for example, Echo "Lake" in Con way has a surface area of 14 acres and a maximum depth of 11 feet, but Island "Pond" in Derry has a surface area of roughly 500 acres and a depth of 80 feet.

DEFINITION OF PONDS AND LAKES
A pond, according to scientist, is any body of water with an area less than two hectares (20, 000 m^2). A lake is a body of water larger than 2 hectares in size.

FOUR KINDS OF PONDS
Make sure you know what you want to achieve from the start and enjoy your water feature-! Ponds with fountains. A fountain pond keeps water clean without the need for a lot of pond plants. Ponds of Waterfall. Water Fall ponds are an excellent way to maximize your outdoor area… Pond-less Waterfalls…Natural Pond.

THE DISTINCTION BETWEEN A POND AND A LAKE
A POND AND A LAKE
A lake is significantly larger than a pond. The sun's beams do not penetrate beneath the lake. A pond, on the other hand, is not deep, and sun rays can readily fail beneath it. These are two primary distinctions between the two.

THE PRIMARY DISTRIBUTIONS BETWEEN A LAKE AND A POND
A Pond is a tiny and confined body of water, where as a lake is huge and open. Even though there are more Ponds than lakes in the world, there are many lakes. Some lakes can reach depth of 4, 000 Feet more although most ponds are shallow.

SIGNIFICANCE OF THE TERM "POND"
In practice, a body of water is referred to as a pond or a lake on an individual basis, as customs vary from location to location and over time. A pond is a vibrant form of the word pound, which means a limiting enclosure. Ponds were once man made and functional, such as stew ponds, mill ponds, and so on.

Geospatial Approaches Modeling for Environmental Water Resources, land use, and Forest Sustainability

WHAT MAKES A POND UNIQUE?

A body of water that is typically smaller than a lake. A pond for fishing. Sometimes used informally of facetiously to refer to the Atlantic Ocean.

TOP 5 POND FACTS

- Ponds and lakes are distinct and similar.
- Healthy Ponds diverse wildlife.
- Ponds form in Unique ways.
- Ponds and lakes do not last forever.
- There are numerous types of Ponds.

CAN WE SAFEGUARD PONDS AND LAKES-!

1. Apply herbicide or algaecide to weeds and algae blooms.
2. Stop nutrient pollution by using natural therapies.
3. Natural Bacteria and Enzyme.
4. Blends prevent Excess Nutrients.
5. Aeration is used to treat the source of pond problems.

POND AND LAKES IMAGES
SHOULD LAKES BE PRESENTED?

Lakes did in addressing the climate catastrophe.

Despite only covering 5-8 percent of the world's land surface, lakes, rivers, and wetlands store 20-30 percent of soil carbon, Protecting and restoring lakes is essential to reducing greenhouse gas emissions and ecosystem and people in adjusting to the effects of climate change.

ISBN: 9798385761821
Imprint: Independently published
COPYRIGHT C EL RAMLY

Geospatial Approaches Modeling for Environmental Water Resources, land use, and Forest Sustainability

SECTION III.   STREAMS AND RIVERS
FLUMES AND RIVERS

Why do Rivers and Streams Exist?
Fresh water that rushes downhill in a channel is called a stream. A stream's channel is called a stream. A Stream's channel has a bed-like bottom and sides with that are referred to as banks. A stream is anybody of moving water, regardless of size. But typically, a wide stream is referred to as river.

THE THIN THAT DISTINGUISH RIVER FROM A STREAM
Even though there are no precise definitions to distinguish these water ways from one another, these water ways from one another, we frequently refer to the largest of these moving bodies of water as a river, the smallest as a Greek, and the in-between rivers as streams.

TRAITS THAT RIVERS AND STREAMS HAVE
There are a few notable variations: Speed: Streams are typically swift and turbulent since they form at higher elevations. RIVERS, on the other hand, are typical calm and slow – moving. Size: Rivers are deeper and have wider banks than streams because they carry more water.

THREE SORTS OF STREAMS EXIST, utilizing physical, hydrological, and biological properties one way to categorize streams to be classified as a permanent intermittent, or ephemeral.

CONNECTIVITY BETWEEN A RIVER AND STREAM
Small creeks are how flowing water initially makes its way downward. Oceans are finally reached via rivers. A lake will form if water flows to an area that is surrounded on all sided by higher ground.

MIGHT A RIVER BE A STREAM?
Smaller, less dense, and more sporadic streams are known as streamlets, brooks, or creeks, while long, broad streams are typically referred to as rivers.

THE SEVEN STREAMS
Five miles west of Hood Rivers, at seven Streams Staging Area, you can access the Post Canyon Trial System, a network of hiking equestrian, mountain biking, and ATV trials. The trails travel across a patch work of public, and forest service properties. The trails are overseen by Hood River Country.

ISBN: 9798385761821
Imprint: Independently published
COPYRIGHT C EL RAMLY

Geospatial Approaches Modeling for Environmental Water Resources, land use, and Forest Sustainability

SECTION IV. DAMS AND RESEVOIRS IN NET LAND
LAND SORT CONSIDERED WET: -
There are many different types of wetlands, including lakes, billabongs, lagoons, rivers, marshes, bogs, mangroves, mudflats, swamps, and flood pains. Most sizable wet land areas frequently have a variety of freshwater system.

EXAMPLE OF A DAM KIND
Hoover Dam is an example of a curving gravity dam built in a narrow gorge across a large river using cutting-edge design ideas is the Hoover Dam, which was constructed on the Colorado River near the Arizona-Nevada border between 1931 and 1936.

IMPACT DAMS HAVE ON RIPARIAN WETLANDS ALONE THE NENIAG RIVER IN NORTHEAST CHINA.
The ISO-KM river reach down stream of the dam has seen a major reduction in riparian wet land areas because of dam construction. The hydrological changes brought on by operation of the dam. Construction. The hydrological changes brought on by operation of the dam have led many former riparian wetlands to become cut off from the river channel and transform into marsh.

DAM'S STRUCTURE
Dams and reservoirs in a wetland. The walled portion of the dam, which opposes the water and permits a controlled amount to flow downstream, is the water retention structure. The face of the dam is the portion of the wall or dump that faces downstream. The crest of the dam is the flat top surface of the structure.

WETLAND' TWO MAIN TYPES
There are five main wet land types in **Cowardian system marine, tidal, lacustrine, palustrine, and riverine.**

ISBN: 9798385761821
Imprint: Independently published
COPYRIGHT C EL RAMLY

Geospatial Approaches Modeling for Environmental Water Resources, land use, and Forest Sustainability

THREE TRAITS WETLANDS HAVE
A wet land is defined as a piece of land with the following characteristics: (1) a predominance of hydrophytic vegetation typically adapted for life in saturated soil conditions; normal support.

DIFFERENCE BETWEEN A DAM FROM A RESEVOIR
A dam is a structure that is built to block or restrict the passage of underground streams of water. In contrast, a reservoir is an open-air storage space (often made of masonry or earth work) where water is gathered and maintained in large quantities so that it can be drawn of and used.

DAM'S THREE ADVENTURES
- Advantages of Big Dams
- Water for drink and use for industries.
- IRRIGATION
- Control of Floods
- Hydro Power Genesis
- Western Navigation
- Recreation

PRIMAL FUNCTION OF DAMS
Dams are constructed so that the appropriate amount of water is present at the appropriate time.
River water rises behind dams to create reservoirs, which are man-made lakes. The water rises behind dams to create reservoirs, which are man – made lakes. The water to buildings and businesses, irrigate land, or did in navigation.

THREE ISSUES DAMS HAVE
Rivers are blocked by dams, which halts fish migration. Dams cause rivers to slow down, creating stagnant back waters that can cause rivers to slow down, creating stagnant back waters that cause algal contamination, low water oxygen levels, and high-water temperatures. And behind them, dams collect masses of mud, sediment, and silt.

THREE DRAW BACKS OF DAMS
Although dams have some positive social effects, they also seriously destroy water ways. On almost all the rivers in our country, dams have diminished fish populations, and changed recreational options.

WETLANDS ARE DESTROYED
Adam's main function is to impound (store) water, wastewater, or other liquid – borne materials for a variety of purposes, including flood control, human water supply, irrigation livestock water supply, energy production, mine tailings containment, recreation, or pollution control. Additionally, a dam serves to raise sea levels, store wastewater, and uproot underprivileged communities.

DAM'S EFFECT ON THE HYDROLOGICAL CYCLE
By Preventing water from flowing through rivers, dams can upset the water cycle's homeostasis.

ISBN: 9798385761821
Imprint: Independently published
COPYRIGHT C EL RAMLY

Geospatial Approaches Modeling for Environmental Water Resources, land use, and Forest Sustainability

DISADVANTAGES OF DAMS DRAW BACKS
Eviction of residents during construction. High levels of greenhouse gases are frequently released by reservoirs regularly disturbs regional ecosystems.
The ground water table is disturbed prevents the flow of water to other nations, states, or areas.

DO DAMS HAVE A BAD IMPACT?
THE WAY RIVERS function is altered by dams. They have the ability to hold sediment, burying fish spawning grounds beneath rock riverbeds. Behind dams, gravel, logs, and other essential components of the food web and environment can also become entrapped. This has detrimental effect on the development and upkeep of more complex habitat (such riffles and pools) downstream.

ADVANTAGES AND DISADVANTAGES OF DAMS!
Beyond their benefits, such as managing stream regimes and so reducing floods, receiving residential and irrigation water from the stored water, and generating energy, dams have a variety of positive and negative environmental effects.

EFFECT OF DAMS ON HUMAN LIFE
The Canals, irrigation plans, roads, power lines, and individual developments that go along with dams have taken away the land and homes of millions more people.
More people in the dammed area no longer have access to fresh water, food sources, and other natural resources.

WHY ARE DAMS USEFUL?
Dams are constructed so that the appropriate amount of water is present at the appropriate location at the appropriate time. River water rises behind dams to create reservoirs, which are man-made lakes. The water that has been stored can be utilized to provide energy, give water to buildings and businesses, irrigate land, or aid in navigation.

ISBN: 9798385761821
Imprint: Independently published
COPYRIGHT C EL RAMLY

Geospatial Approaches Modeling for Environmental Water Resources, land use, and Forest Sustainability

SECTION V: TREATMENT OF WASTEWATER AND DRINKING WATER

After passing through the sewage treatment facility, it is further processed using cutting-edge chemical, biological, and physical methods in a second plant (and occasionally a third). The drinking supply system or the natural system is then directly, provided with the water (rivers, lakes, aquifers, or reservoirs).

PRODUCING DRINKING WATER FROM WASTEWATER

Potable water reuse is the process of utilizing treated wastewater to produce drinking water. Re using potable water gives a region another way to diversify its supply of water resources.

WASTEWATER TREATMENT

A technique called wastewater treatment is used to clean up impurities from wastewater and turn it into an effluent that can be reintroduced to the water cycle. The wastewater is used, reused, or has on acceptable impact on the environment after it is added back into the water cycle (Called Water Reclamation).

WASTEWATER MIGHT BE MADE DRINKABLE

The practice of further treating wastewater that has already been treated at a sewage facility is known as direct potable reuse. When the water is clean enough to drink, it is immediately redeposited into a drinking water distribution system, typically much closer to the location where it is most required.

EXIT METHODS FOR TREATING WATER

PRIMARY (SOLID REMOVAL), Secondary (bacterial decomposition) and Territory (Chemical treatment) are three stages of waste treatment (Extra filtration).

PROCESS IN TREATMENT OF WASTEWATER TREATMENT IN ADVANCE

Pumping, screening, and Primary Treatment. The wastewater then moves into primary setting tanks, where the water flow is slowed down.
Secondary Therapy Aeration and final setting; disinfection; sludge treatment, waste-to-energy; and sludge treatment.

TOP 7 WATER TECHNIQUES

Flocculation or Coagulation.
Coagulation is the process of combining raw or untreated water with liquid Aluminum sulfate, alum, and/or polymer. Sedimentation after treatment, flocs and water are deposited in basins for sedimentation. Filtration, disinfection, sludge, drying, fluoridation, pH correction, and other process.

TWO PRIMARY METHODS OF TREATMENT WATER

Water passes through a filter membrane with incredibly small pores during ultrafiltration. This filter only permits water and other small molecules to pass through (such as salts and tiny, charged molecules) Another filtering technique for removing extra particles from water is to reverse osmosis.

ISBN: 9798385761821
Imprint: Independently published
COPYRIGHT C EL RAMLY

Geospatial Approaches Modeling for Environmental Water Resources, land use, and Forest Sustainability

FOUR FORMS OF PURIFICATION ARE EMPLOYED TO WASTE WATER TREATMENT FACILITIES?

Physical process like filtration, sedimentation, and distillation, biological processing like slow sand filters or biology active carbon chemical process like flocculation and chlorination, and the use of electromagnetic radiation like ultraviolet light and just a few of the techniques used.

KEY GOALS WATER TREATMENT SERUE

Water treatment is a procedure that combines many operations (physical), chemical, physicochemical, and biological), with the objective of reducing or eliminating contaminants qualities in water.

DIIFERENT KINDS OF WASTEWATER TREATMENT EXIST

The Primary, secondary, and tertiary water treatment process.

WATER TREATMENT IN REGARD OF ASPECT IS CRUCIAL

As much suspended solids as possible must be eliminated during wastewater treatment before the left-over water, known effluent, is released back into the environment. The Oxygen that is animals is depleted during the break down of solid matter.

OUTCOME OF THE TREATMENT OF WASTEWATER

Protecting people and the environment from the hazardous and destructive substances contained in wastewater is primary objective of waste water treatment facilities. Because the natural process of purifying water is overburdened, water treatment facilities were created to accelerate the natural process.

ISBN: 9798385761821
Imprint: Independently published
COPYRIGHT C EL RAMLY

Geospatial Approaches Modeling for Environmental Water Resources, land use, and Forest Sustainability

PART III. LAND USE

I. COMMON USES OF LAND
Residential, agricultural, recreational, transit, and commercial land use are the five main categories. While many choices impacting local projects are made at the municipal, managing the different uses of property is done through collaboration involving state, federal, and municipal organizations.

ILLUSTRATION OF LAND USE
Land use does not refer to the type of ground cover; rather, it describes the use that is made of the habitat, or recreation. As an illustration, a recreational land use might take place in a forest, shrubland, grassland, or on a well-kept lawn.

II. IMPORTANCE OF LAND USE
SIGNIFICANCE THAT LANDS USE HAVE
THEREFORE, the necessity to meet these objectives particularly, logically, and within a technical framework, is the root of land-use planning. It is an essential step in the integrated development planning process and considers their spatial and land use component.

III. TYPES OF LANDS
Land use categories include those for agriculture, industry, commerce, housing, recreation, and transportation.

IV. LAND USE CATEGORY
DIFFERENT TYPES OF LAND USE
A land – use classification is a categorization that offers details on the sorts of human activities engaged in land usage as well as land cover. Additionally, it can make it easier to evaluate the environmental effects on the land and possible or alternative uses for it.

V. FOUR FACTORS OF LAND USE
Environmental elements like soil qualities, climate, topography, and vegetarian undoubtedly have an impact on how land is used.

VI. ELEMENTS OF LAND USE PLANTING
Technically speaking, the factors that go into planning are in the quantity of land that is available and its tenure; the quality, potential productivity, and suitability of the land; the technology; and the needs and standards of living of the people.

Geospatial Approaches Modeling for Environmental Water Resources, land use, and Forest Sustainability

ANNEX
APPLICATION OF GIS AND REMOTE SENSING FOR THE FOREST

ISBN: 9798385761821
Imprint: Independently published
COPYRIGHT C EL RAMLY

> **Geospatial Approaches Modeling for Environmental Water Resources, land use, and Forest Sustainability**

Applications of GIS and Remote Sensing for the Forest Resource Monitoring System including Carbon Stock

5TH. February. 2023

SHAHINAZ EL RAMLY
ESSDS EXPERT
Forest Inventory/Project Coordinator

ISBN: 9798385761821
Imprint: Independently published
COPYRIGHT C EL RAMLY

Geospatial Approaches Modeling for Environmental Water Resources, land use, and Forest Sustainability

2. Challenges in PNG

1. Forest Monitoring Is Required
2. Forest Monitoring Project Activities
3. PNGFA's Conceptual Framework for Forest Monitoring
4. Analysis of Forest Area Change
5. Remote Sensing Field Monitoring

1. A national scale base map of forest resources is created and used.
2. A GIS/Database for national-scale forest resources has been created and is in use.
3. A carbon stock monitoring system for forests is developed and demonstrated.

Forest Base map   Estimation/Modeling

$R^2 = 0.8345$

Satellite Imagery

ISBN: 9798385761821
Imprint: Independently published
COPYRIGHT C EL RAMLY

Geospatial Approaches Modeling for Environmental Water Resources, land use, and Forest Sustainability

Project Activities for Forest Monitoring

Concept of Forest Monitoring for REDD+

Field verification for Remote Sensing

Training and trial of forest carbon survey

Forest carbon estimation for FRA2015

Carbon analysis using airborne data.

µ

ISBN: 9798385761821
Imprint: Independently published
COPYRIGHT C EL RAMLY

Geospatial Approaches Modeling for Environmental Water Resources, land use, and Forest Sustainability

Activities

ISBN: 9798385761821
Imprint: Independently published
COPYRIGHT C EL RAMLY

Geospatial Approaches Modeling for Environmental Water Resources, land use, and Forest Sustainability

Forest Area Change Analysis

Optical satellite image (RapidEye) 2022

Forest Area Change Analysis
Cloud free satellite image (ALOS/PALSAR) 2022

Forest Area Change Analysis
Cloud free satellite image (ALOS/PALSAR) 2022

ISBN: 9798385761821
Imprint: Independently published
COPYRIGHT C EL RAMLY

Geospatial Approaches Modeling for Environmental Water Resources, land use, and Forest Sustainability

ISBN: 9798385761821
Imprint: Independently published
COPYRIGHT C EL RAMLY

Geospatial Approaches Modeling for Environmental Water Resources, land use, and Forest Sustainability

FIELD VERIFICIATION OF REMOTE SENSING

ISBN: 9798385761821
Imprint: Independently published
COPYRIGHT C EL RAMLY

Geospatial Approaches Modeling for Environmental Water Resources, land use, and Forest Sustainability

SOIL PLOTTING

SATELLITE RADAR

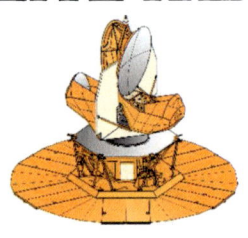

ISBN: 9798385761821
Imprint: Independently published
COPYRIGHT C EL RAMLY

Geospatial Approaches Modeling for Environmental Water Resources, land use, and Forest Sustainability

FOREST MAPPING GIS

Purpose To train relevant PNGFA personnel on how to conduct field verification using GPS and GIS.

ESSDS RESEARCH 2022

ISBN: 9798385761821
Imprint: Independently published
COPYRIGHT C EL RAMLY

Geospatial Approaches Modeling for Environmental Water Resources, land use, and Forest Sustainability

PART IV. FOREST SUSTAINABILITY

SECTION I: TOWARD FOREST SUSTAINABILITY
What exactly does the term "sustainable Forestry" mean?
Create protected regions and protect biodiversity.
Protect High Conversation Value Forests (HCV) and stop forest conversion.
Have a management strategy in place and harvest when necessary. The role tree plantations is important use low-impact logging methods.

THREE ELEMENTS MAKE UP SUSTAINABLE FORESTRY
THERE ARE ELEMENTS COMPONENTS OF SUSTAINABLE FORESTRY
THERE IS ESSENTIAL COMPONENT OF SUSTAINABLE FORESTRY
ENVIRONMENTALLY SUSTAINABLE WARMING. SAFEGUARDS Biodiversity and ensures the long-term availability of renewable resources.
Economic Sustainability, social Sustainability.

SIGNIFICANCE THAT MAINTAINING FORESTS HAVE.
Sustainably managed Forests provide significant ecosystem services, such as carbon sequestration biodiversity preservation, and the safeguarding of water resources, in addition to wood and non-wood forest products.

SUSTAINABLE FOREST MANAGEMENT OUTLOOLK PRACTICE SELECTIVE LOGGING, which is the process of removing specific trees while maintaining the balance of the wood land, is one illustration of sustainable Forest management in addition, expanding forest lands by planting trees protecting existing forests, and giving young trees time to mature as example.

GOALS OF SUSTAINABLE FOREST DEVELOPMENT
SUSTAINABLE FOREST DEVELOPMENT PURSUE!
Goal is one of the Sustainable Development Agenda is to "reserve", restore, and promote sustainable use of terrestrial ecosystems, sustainably manage forests, battle desertification, and to stop, reverse, and otherwise significantly reduce land degradation and biodiversity loss.

SECTION II: FOREST POLICY WICKED PROBLEM – A MULTIDISICIPLINARY STRATEGY IN THE STUDY OF FOREST LANDSCAPES
IS THE LOSS OF FORESTS A WICKED PROBLEM
According to research coauthor and standard Earth professor Eric Lambin, deforestation is a terrible problem that defies simple fixes.
"A wide range of factors, including the geographic setting and stake holders with various objectives land uses, and values, influence targets, methods, and progress.

DIFFICULTIES THAT ARISE WHEN TRYING TO MANAGE ALIVE RESOURCES LIKE A FOREST
Depletion brought on by natural. (Files and infestations) for human activities (clear, cutting, burning and land conversion) as well as monitoring of health and growth for efficient economic exploitation and conservation are the key challenges to forest management.

SECTION III. MINI FOREST REVOLUTION
SMALL – SALE FOREST REVOLUTION IN "Mini Forest Revolution," author Hannah Lewis demonstrates how organizations all over the world are restoring devasted areas to defense forests that create green spaces and aid in reducing global warming by absorbing carbon, thanks to a forestation technique developed by Japanese botanist Akira Miyawaki.

TINY FORESTS EXACTLY
MINI-Forests are, as their name suggests, little patches of Forest that are frequently found in metropolitan environment. Three saplings are planted every square meter, which is a fair higher density than in typical forests. Thus, cluster nevertheless, still derives adequate room for the trees to develop.

ISBN: 9798385761821
Imprint: Independently published
COPYRIGHT C EL RAMLY

Geospatial Approaches Modeling for Environmental Water Resources, land use, and Forest Sustainability

MIYAWAKI METHOD FOR A LITTLE FOREST REVOLUTION ENTAIL

Akira Miyawaki, a Japanese botanist, developed the Miyawaki Method, a novel strategy for reforestation, which Lewis introduces in Mini-Forest Revolution.

She illustrates how incredibly small forests – as small as six parking spaces – grow quickly and use significantly more biodiversity's than those that are established using traditional techniques.

THE ADVANTAGES THAT TINY FOREST OFFER

TINY FOREST can help people feel more well – rounded by introducing them to the surrounding natural environment. They provide a spot to unwind, see nature, and access to information.

CREATION OF A MINIATURE FOREST

THE MIYWAKI method for creating a miniature forest is to determine the soil texture and calculate the biomass Step 1.
Step 2: Decide which trees species to plant.:
Step 3: Decide the Forest
Step 4: Setting up the space.
Step 5: Plant the trees.
Step 6: Maintain the forest for three years.

ADVANTAGES MIYAWAKI FOREST OFFER

The soil is well shielded. Effectively reducing erosion and the possibility of flooding. For biodiversity, forests are in excellent environment. Significant amount of Co_x that are no longer in the atmosphere are stored in forests.

HOW BIG A LITTLER TREE FOREST

What makes a Tiny Forest unique? A tiny forest is a very small, densely planted forest the size of a tennis course created with the help of Dr. Miyawaki's planting technique in Japan. The forest is 30 times denser than a conventionally planted forest and consists of 600 trees of a variety of nature species.

TREES USED IN MIYAWKI FOREST

SIXTEEN Fast growing trees namely Pong Amia pinnata, Thespesia populnea, Terminalia catapa, Alibizia saman, Holoptelea intergrifolia, Azedaracta indica, Melia azedarach, Petroccirpum, Azibzia lebbeck, Spatodea campanulate, Adenanthera pavonine, Swietenia macrophylla, Fiscusim.

ADVANTAGES OF FOREST ROSTERATION

Better local climate regulation, enhanced flood and erosion control, a wider range and greater accessibility of food and non-food goods, and higher employment opportunities for the local population are all advantages.

ADVANTAGES OF FOREST RESTORATION

Better local climate regulation, enhanced flood and erosion control, a wider range and greater accessibility of flood and non-food and non-food goods, and higher employment opportunities for the local population are all advantages.

ISBN: 9798385761821
Imprint: Independently published
COPYRIGHT C EL RAMLY

Geospatial Approaches Modeling for Environmental Water Resources, land use, and Forest Sustainability

BENEFITS OF REFORESTATION
Reforestation benefits ecosystems and the earth in a number of ways. Benefits include increased soil fertility, increased biodiversity in wildlife habitats, and carbon sequestration.

IV. BOOK RECOMMENDATION
THE GHOST FOREST: Racists, Radicals, and Real Estate in the California Red woods.

STORY OF THE BOOK

"

THE Authoritative account of the California red woods' discovery and exploitation, as related by a campaigner who struggled to defend them against those who wanted to destroy them.

The renowned red woods of California are visited by millions of tourists each year from around the globe. However, few people who crane their necks to see tops of the tallest trees in the world are aware of how unlikely it is that any these final, remote stands of enormous trees will ever again stand. In this compelling historical biography, renowned red wood activist and journalist Greg.

SECTION V.: PLANNING OF FOREST MANAGEMENT
A commitment to safeguarding various forest values in the managed region must be outlines in a forest management plan, which often covers a span of several decades. Moreover, Describe the areas as desired future state for the forest values.

THE TEAM "FOREST MANAGEMENT
Planning and putting into effect strategies for the care and use of forests to achieve environment, economic, social, and culture goals is the process of forest management. It covers. the management of both natural and planted forest from administrative, economic, legal, social, technical, and scientific standpoint.

PURPOSE OF LOCAL FOREST MANAGEMENT STRATEGY
The MMSP's goal is to integrate bio-physical, environmental, socioeconomic, technical and development policy issues for sustainable forest management and the best possible fulfillment of local opportunity/societal requirements from local forest.

ISBN: 9798385761821
Imprint: Independently published
COPYRIGHT C EL RAMLY

Geospatial Approaches Modeling for Environmental Water Resources, land use, and Forest Sustainability

SIGNIFICANCE OF MANAGING FORESTS

Sustainability managed forests provide significant ecosystem services, such as carbon sequestration, biodiversity preservation, and the safeguarding of water resources, in addition to wood and non-wood forest products.

ISBN: 9798385761821
Imprint: Independently published
COPYRIGHT C EL RAMLY

Geospatial Approaches Modeling for Environmental Water Resources, land use, and Forest Sustainability

PART V: PROMULAGTION LAWS
SECTION I: PROMULGATION LAWS

LAW ON WATER ALLOCATION
What is water distribution?
Water allocations are the percentages of water that can be taken against an entitlement each year. Allocations vary depending on whether this year is wet or dry. In a rainy year, for example, crops are, watered directly by rain fall, requiring less water for irrigation.

WATCH RESOURCES ALLOCATION AND MANAGEMENT
Water resource allocation affects has access to water resources, as well as how, when and where. It has a direct impact on the value (economic, ecological and socio culture) that individuals and society place on water resources.

STATE THAT HAS THE BEST WATER RIGHTS
According to the score card, California was the highest scoring state – the state with the most advanced policies on water efficiency, conservation, sustainability, and accessibility. TEXAS, ARIZON, GEORGIA, WASINGTON, NEW YORK, NEVADA, NEW HAMPSHIRE, COLORADO AND MINNESTOTA TRAILED CALIFORNIA.

SIGNIFICANCE OF WATER RIGHTS
Water rights regulations aim to ensure that a water user will have access to water in the future. Water rights are based on a priority system that determines who can continue to take water there is insufficient water to next all needs.

IS IT POSSIBLE TO HAVE CONSTITUTIONAL RIGHT TO WATER?
The federal government of the United States does not acknowledge the human right to water, but several provisions of federal law encourage specific components of the right.

WATER RIGHTS STATED BY THE UNITED NATION
The United Nation General Assembly expressly recognized the human right to water and sanitation on July 28, 2010, through Resolution 64/292, and acknowledged that clean water and sanitation are vital to the realization fo all human rights.

'Article 21'

21. Life and personal liberty protection No one shall be deprived of his life or personal liberty except in accordance with the legal procedure.

ISBN: 9798385761821
Imprint: Independently published
COPYRIGHT C EL RAMLY

Geospatial Approaches Modeling for Environmental Water Resources, land use, and Forest Sustainability

WATER IS A HUMAN RIGHT OR COMMODITY

Anyone making a profit from something we cannot live without not permitted. Water according to economists, is commodity. The United Nations General Assembly adopted a resolution in July 2010 recognizing the right to safe drinking water and sanitation as a fundamental human right.

IS WATER A PUBLIC OR PRIVATE GOOD?

Water is a private good whether it is used at home, in a factory, or on a farm. When water is left in place, whether for transportation, leisure, or aquatic habitat, it's considered a public good.

' 'Article 29'

Article29 of the Indian Institution 1949

Many Interests must be protected. (1) Any group of citizens residing in India's territory or any portion of it who speak, write, or practice a separate language, script, or culture has the right to preserve it.

' 'Article 31'

31 A, 31 B and 31 C of the constitution of 1949

Originally one of the seven essential rights was the right to property, which stated that no one shall be stripped of his property except by authority law.

ISBN: 9798385761821
Imprint: Independently published
COPYRIGHT C EL RAMLY

Geospatial Approaches Modeling for Environmental Water Resources, land use, and Forest Sustainability

SECTION II: LAW INACTED BY FEDERAL STATE REGIONAL

WHAT IS THE 1965 FEDERAL WATER QUALITY ACT?

FEDERALREGIONAL STATE, AND LOCAL WATER MANAGEMENT LAWS.
The Water Quality Act increased yearly Federal. Construction Funds from $ 150 million, promoted multi – community and large-scale construction projects, consolidated accountability within federal administrations, and provided clear, innovative Water Quality Violation Standards.

FEDERAL AGENCIES THAT ARE CONCERNED ABOUT WATER
Programs of the federal and state Governments Reclamation Bureau Agency. Water Resources Division of the Geological Survey National Environmental information Agency.
Water Resources National Institute.
The United States Geological Survey's National Water Assessment Program.
"Google Definition"

CURRENT FEDERAL STATUE IN THE UNITED STATES THAT GOVERNS WATER POLLUTION
This statue became known as the clean water Act Once it was enacted by federal, regional, state, and local water management authorities (CAN) Act is the primary statute governing pollution management and water Quality in the nation's water ways. The CAN's goal is to restore and maintain the chemical, physical, and biological integrity of the country's water (33. US. C. 1251) "Google Definition"

What role do state federal water projects play?
The SWP's major function is water supply distribution and flood control, but also driver's numerous other benefits, including power generation. Activities for recreation. Et seq (1972). The clean water Act (CWA) defines the basic structure for regulating pollution discharges into US water as well as surface water Quality Criteria.

ACT "2022"
What exactly is the water Act 2022?
Water and Water rights should not be traded in commodities futures contracts. The proposed measure would add "water" to the commodity Exchange Act's current list of prohibitions.

SECTION 33 OF THE WATER ACT 1974
Section 33. Authority of the Board to file an application in court to halt suspected pollution of water in streams of wells. Section 3A. Directional authority.

LOCAL WATER MANAGEMENT
LOCAL WATER MANAGEMENT EXACTLY / LOCAL WATER ADMINISTRATION. Country Governments, as a general-purpose level of government, are particularly positioned to combine many land use decisions which local goals for surface and ground water preservation and management.
Water management is the responsibility of countries.

ISBN: 9798385761821
Imprint: Independently published
COPYRIGHT C EL RAMLY

Geospatial Approaches Modeling for Environmental Water Resources, land use, and Forest Sustainability

IMPORTANCE OF WATER MANAGEMENT

Water management is crucial because influences future irrigation expectations. Water management is the administration of water resources in accordance with established policies and laws. Water formerly a plentiful natural resource, is becoming increasingly valuable as a result of droughts and abuse.

ISBN: 9798385761821
Imprint: Independently published
COPYRIGHT C EL RAMLY

Geospatial Approaches Modeling for Environmental Water Resources, land use, and Forest Sustainability

CONFLICTS OVER WATER
&
XYZ SOLUTION

What is the source of the water conflict?

Water disputes arise when demand for water resources and drinkable water exceeds availability, when control over access and allocation of water is disputed or when water management institutions are weak or non-existent.

What is the solution to the water problem?

Dams and reservoirs, rainwater harvesting, aqueducts, desalination, water reuse, and water conservation are all solutions to water scarcity.

What can governments do to address the water crisis?

Water management that is equitable and prudent, Governments can ensure the long-term sustainability of freshwater resource use by: establishing maximum sustainable limits for water use and pollution in river basins and aquifers to achieve an adequate balance between water people and nature.

ISBN: 9798385761821
Imprint: Independently published
COPYRIGHT C EL RAMLY

Geospatial Approaches Modeling for Environmental Water Resources, land use, and Forest Sustainability

EPILOGUE

THREE KINDS OF GEOSPATIAL DATA

ATTRIBUTES AND VECTORS Points, lines, and polygons are examples of descriptive information about a location. Point clouds are groups of chartered points that can be recons textured as 3D objects. Raster and satellite imagery's High + Resolution aerial photographs of our globe.

What is a geospatial approach?

Geographic information is collected, analyzed, and stored using geospatial technologies. It uses software to geographic planes and assess the impact of human activity. Geographic information Systems (GIS) combine map and databases regarding natural occurrences and socioeconomic trends using digital software.

What are the four most important elements of geospatial technologies?

A functional GIS consists of five major components: hardware, software, data, people, and techniques. The machine on which a GIS runs is referred to as its hardware, GIS software now runs on a wide range of hardware, to stand-alone on networked desktop computers.

What are the different forms of GIS data models?

Within a GIS you will frequently employ two types of data models: Vector. (Points, lines, and polygons) (made up of "pixels") (made up of "pixels")

What are the five steps of the geographic approach?

Step one is to ask. Approaching a problem spatially entails framing the question from a location-based standpoint.
Step Two: obtain.
Step five: examine.
Step four: analyze.
Step five: Act…. A Better understanding of the Results.

What are the five spatial concepts?

Queries and reasoning, measurements, transformation, descriptive summaries, optimization, and hypothesis testing are the six forms of spatial analysis.

What are the three common geospatial technologies in agriculture?

Farmers can assess differences in soil Quality for growing crops using geospatial technologies such as GPS, GIS, and Land Sat Satellite photography.

ISBN: 9798385761821
Imprint: Independently published
COPYRIGHT C EL RAMLY

Geospatial Approaches Modeling for Environmental Water Resources, land use, and Forest Sustainability

What exactly is the geospatial method?

A hands-on course designed to teach forestry students the fundamentals of geoinformatics. They will be introduced to spatial data processing including the creation of high-quality maps cartographic representations of geographical space, as well as analysis.

What is the difference between GIS and geospatial?

ESSENTIALLY, GIS refers to a single, specific technology, while geospatial by itself is a **Catchall** adjective that encompasses a wide range of technologies and scientific fields relating to geography.

ISBN: 9798385761821
Imprint: Independently published
COPYRIGHT C EL RAMLY

Geospatial Approaches Modeling for Environmental Water Resources, land use, and Forest Sustainability

ADDENDUM

ISBN: 9798385761821
Imprint: Independently published
COPYRIGHT C EL RAMLY

Geospatial Approaches Modeling for Environmental Water Resources, land use, and Forest Sustainability

South Africa Science

Copyright © Shahinaz El Ramly
All Rights ® are reserved, no copy or deform is licensed, not to be copied, reproduced, or stored in any retrieval system, or transmitted, in any form or by any means, electronic, mechanical, photocopying, recording or otherwise, without prior written permission of the copyright author.
Design by Shahinaz El Ramly
Reproduction by KDP AMAZON
Photographs @ Pixa
Cairo, Egypt
Frist Published in 2022

ISBN: 9798371504852
Imprint: Independently published

ISBN: 9798385761821
Imprint: Independently published
COPYRIGHT C EL RAMLY

Geospatial Approaches Modeling for Environmental Water Resources, land use, and Forest Sustainability

SOUTH AFRICA IS THIS

What human traits are present in South Africa?
The majority of black South Africans are friendly, tenacious, tolerant, creative, and charismatic people. They are also incredibly socially diverse, with populations from many different tribal groups (such as the Zulu, Xhosa, Sotho, Tswana, Tsonga, Swazi, and Venda tribes).

How do the guys in South Africa fare?
From 2011 to 2021, the South African population was measured according to sexual orientation. In 2021, there were approximately 30.48 million female residents of South Africa, compared to approximately 29.56 million male residents.

What is the best way to sum up South Africa?
Since the formal end of apartheid (Afrikaans: "apartness," or racial segregation) in 1994, South Africa, the southernmost country on the African continent, has been a popular tourism destination because of its diverse topography, stunning natural beauty, and cultural diversity.

How is dating a South African like?
Although South African dates are frequently straightforward, women still value chivalry, bravery, and gentlemanly behavior in men. They adore a man they can flaunt to their loved ones, after all. And the males provide without a doubt. They are typically kind and conventional, if not a tad sport obsessed.

Who arrived in South Africa first?
African Australopithecus
Australopithecus africanus is the first hominid known to have lived in southern Africa. A. robustus is believed to have first been locally documented around 2 million years ago, around the same time when Homo (? developed into Homo) displaced it.

South Africa is what race?
Black Africans make up three-fourths of the population, including the Zulu, Xhosa, Sotho, and Tswana; most of the remaining people are of European, mixed-race, or South Asian ancestry.

Can a man from South Africa have two wives?
In South Africa, a man may wed more than one woman, but a woman may not have more than one husband. Politicians are presently debating granting women the same rights as men, including the right to marry. In South Africa, polyandry is not permitted but polygyny is.

What distinguishes South Africans as unique?
The inhabitants of South Africa are from a remarkably broad range of ethnic origins and cultures. That is what makes South Africa such a fascinating and distinctive destination. Due to the wide variety of cultures and religions present there, South Africa is well known as the "rainbow nation."

ISBN: 9798385761821
Imprint: Independently published
COPYRIGHT C EL RAMLY

Geospatial Approaches Modeling for Environmental Water Resources, land use, and Forest Sustainability

What characterizes the African?
African personalities are inherently dynamic and capable of self-realization in a variety of contexts, including interpersonal and societal interactions as well as domestic and foreign policy.

What characteristics characterize South Africans?
South Africa is famed for its safaris, breathtaking coastline, braais, and wine. Its prominence stems from apartheid, its turbulent past, and the legendary Nelson Mandela, the country's first black president.

The finest place to live is South Africa?
It is regarded as one of the most diverse nations in the world and provides a wealth of fascinating prospects for expats. The affordable cost of living, incredible wildlife, and pleasant climate are just a few of the reasons why British adventurers love South Africa so much.

WHO ARE THE INHABITANTS OF SOUTH AFRICA?
Around 81% of South Africans are black, while 9% are colored, 8% are white, and 3% are Indian. After Nigeria, Ethiopia, and Egypt, the population of the nation ranks as the fourth largest in Africa and the 25th-largest in the world. Go back to the introduction.

What are the prevailing gender roles in South Africa?
It is believed that a variety of ethnic groups in South Africa hold deep-rooted attitudes about gender roles, the majority of which are founded on the idea that women there are less significant or deserving of power than men. Some believe that traditional social structures in Africa are male-centric and male-dominated.

Are males from South Africa uncut?
Customs. 92% of men in North Africa and 62% of men in Sub-Saharan Africa have undergone circumcision. In contrast to the southern regions of Africa, where it is more frequently performed in newborns as a rite of passage into manhood, it is primarily conducted for religious reasons in western and northern portions of Africa.

What draws people to South Africa?
Many would-be travelers find "Africa" to have a seductive allure, and South Africa's reputation as a place that provides such a wide range of breathtaking vacations and experiences throughout the year, combined with its First World infrastructure, continues to draw more and more visitors to its excellent beaches.

Do people in South Africa speak English?
With eleven official languages, South Africa is a country with a fully bilingual population. The percentage of South Africans who speak English as their primary language is only around 9%. However, South African English, or SAE, although being a minority language, has a significant impact on South African society.

Do we have a billionaire in South Africa?
The 18 African billionaires come from seven different nations and are all seasoned veterans. Five billionaires reside in South Africa, five in Egypt, three each in Nigeria and Morocco, and two each in Nigeria and Egypt.

ISBN: 9798385761821
Imprint: Independently published
COPYRIGHT C EL RAMLY

Geospatial Approaches Modeling for Environmental Water Resources, land use, and Forest Sustainability

What are the three most valued in South Africa? mage outcome?
Gold, platinum, ore, and automobile

What did South Africa invent?
Some of the firsts in the globe can be attributed to South Africa. The CAT scan, the first heart transplant, and the speed gun all on the list. Where would you expect to find the creators of the CAT scan, the "speed gun" used in cricket ovals around the globe, or the first coal-to-oil refinery in the world?

In South Africa, how do you express "I love you"?
- There are 11 official languages in South Africa.
- English: I cherish you.
- Afrikaans: I'm happy for you.
- Keagorata in Sepedi.
- Niyakutanda speaks IsiNdebele.
- Ndiyakuthanda in IsiXhosa.
- Ngiyakuthanda in IsiZulu
- Keagorata Sesotho
- Ngiyakutsandza SiSwati.

Does South Africa experience snow?
Snowfall is uncommon; it has occurred in May 1956, August 1962, June 1964, September 1981, August 2006 (light), on June 27, 2007, when up to 10 centimeters (3.9 in) of snow accumulated in the southern suburbs, and most recently.

Why do individuals decide to remain in South Africa?
Most days of the year, South Africans see crystal-clear blue skies and plenty of sunshine. Durban experiences year-round tropical weather, although winter days in Cape Town can reach temperatures of up to 25C. Summer rains do fall in Johannesburg, but they never persist long enough to ruin your outdoor activities.

Who moves to South Africa and why?
Since labor in South Africa is so inexpensive, expatriates are frequently offered substantial incomes, which allows them to maintain a good quality of life and hire domestic help on a part- or full-time basis. Alcohol and eating out are also regarded as inexpensive.

What kind of people live in South Africa?
Black South Africans are friendly, tolerant, patient, creative, and charming people. They are also highly culturally varied, with people from several tribal groups living there (for example, the Zulu, Xhosa, Sotho, Tswana, Tsonga, Swazi and Venda tribes).

The finest place to live is South Africa?
It is regarded as one of the most diverse nations in the world and provides a wealth of fascinating prospects for expats. The affordable cost of living, incredible wildlife, and pleasant climate are just a few of the reasons why British adventurers love South Africa so much.

ISBN: 9798385761821
Imprint: Independently published
COPYRIGHT C EL RAMLY

Geospatial Approaches Modeling for Environmental Water Resources, land use, and Forest Sustainability

Which race is wealthier in South Africa?
Even though black South Africans make up most of the workforce, white South Africans earn more than three times as much on average, according to data made available by CNN.

What is South Africa's coolest feature?
The Vredefort Dome in the town of Parys is the oldest meteor crater in the world, and it is in South Africa. A UNESCO World Heritage Site, the location. The Roves Rail in South Africa is regarded as the world's most opulent train. The highest commercial bungi jump in the world, which is in South Africa, is 710 feet high.

What do people wear in South Africa?
Even at most restaurants, the dress code is typically casual. However, there are a few more upscale city hotels and eateries where you might feel more at ease wearing a smart casual dress.

Five things to know about South Africa
- The only nation in the world to have three capitals.
- In South Africa, you can go swimming among penguins.
- The second-largest fruit grower in the world is South Africa.
- One of the oldest mountains in the world is the Table Mountain.
- The tallest waterfall in the world is Tugela Falls.

What is Africa's nickname?
The old name of Africa was Alkebulan, according to Dr. cheikh Anah Diop in Kemetic History of Afrika. "Garden of Eden" or "mother of mankind" is Alkebu-lan. The oldest and only word with indigenous origins is alkebulan. The Moors, Nubians, Numidians, Khart-Haddans (Carthaginians), and Ethiopians all made use of it.

Why is South Africa so adored by people?
"A world in one country" has been used to describe South Africa. It offers modern cities, a rainbow nation with a wide variety of cultural traditions, breathtaking landscape, and, of course, the opportunity to go on a Big Five safari. South Africa has everything!

Why is South Africa so significant globally?
South Africa plays a significant economic and political influence on the continent as the region's most developed economy and one of the continent's strongest democracies.

Why is South Africa so incredible?
'Unmatched wildlife and mountains, whales and waterfalls, architecture and antiquity, the world's most beautiful city, the world's most breathtaking spring, and a host of natural treasures make South Africa "The Most Beautiful Country in The World,"' according to a Buzzfeed article about the country.

What is Africa's nickname?
The old name of Africa was Alkebulan, according to Dr. cheikh Anah Diop in Kemetic History of Afrika. "Garden of Eden" or "mother of mankind" is Alkebu-lan. The oldest and only word with indigenous origins is alkebulan. The Moors, Nubians, Numidians, Khart-Haddans (Carthaginians), and Ethiopians all made use of it.

ISBN: 9798385761821
Imprint: Independently published
COPYRIGHT C EL RAMLY

Geospatial Approaches Modeling for Environmental Water Resources, land use, and Forest Sustainability

Is it a decent place to live in South Africa?
Living in South Africa has numerous benefits. It is a beautiful country with unrivaled natural beauty, varied cultures, delectable cuisine, and activities to suit any taste. Additionally, its people, businesses, and towns all exude a warm wamkelekile (welcome).

In what does South Africa excel?
Several different minerals are abundant in South Africa. The nation has reserves of iron ore, platinum, manganese, chromium, copper, uranium, silver, beryllium, and titanium in addition to diamond and gold.

Is South Africa a pleasant nation?
Each year, South Africa, its towns, and its people take home many international honors. Cape Town was rated the best city in the world to visit, and South Africa was ranked as the fifth most beautiful country in the world in 2017. Our beaches rank among the best.

Why is South Africa so adored by people?
"A world in one country" has been used to describe South Africa. It offers modern cities, a rainbow nation with a wide variety of cultural traditions, breathtaking landscape, and, of course, the opportunity to go on a Big Five safari. South Africa has everything!

Why is South Africa so significant globally?
South Africa plays a significant economic and political influence on the continent as the region's most developed economy and one of the continent's strongest democracies.

What distinguishes South Africa the most?
The only nation in the world with three capital cities is South Africa. A statue of Nelson Mandela that is larger than life may be found in Pretoria's Union Buildings. The capital cities of South Africa are in three separate places. This is meant to symbolize the three divisions of the South African government.

South Africa: affluent or impoverished?
South Africa's economy is the third largest in Africa and the continent's most industrialized, technologically advanced, and diversified. One of just eight countries in Africa with an upper-middle-income economy is South Africa.

What is the South African culture?
The South African culture
Due to the wide variety of cultures and religions present there, South Africa is well known as the "rainbow nation." Zulu, Xhosa, Pedi, Tswana, Ndebele, Khoisan, Hindu, Muslim, and Afrikaner people are just a handful of the ethnic groups who call South Africa home.

Which nation is the richest in the world?
As of 2021, the United States has the largest GDP in the entire planet. With a $17.734 trillion GDP, China is the second-richest country in the world.

ISBN: 9798385761821
Imprint: Independently published
COPYRIGHT C EL RAMLY

Geospatial Approaches Modeling for Environmental Water Resources, land use, and Forest Sustainability

What type of food is popular in South Africa?
In South Africa, you must consume biltong and droewors before leaving. Before refrigerators were created, South Africa's traditional tribes employed dry curing to preserve meat. Examples include Boerewors, Cape Malay curry, Malva pudding, Chakalaka & pap, Braai/Shisa nyama, Bunny chow, and Amarula Don Pedro.

Exactly how strong is South Africa?
South Africa is now regarded as the 26th-strongest military power in the world, up from 32nd in 2022.
10 biggest military spenders (Defense Budget) Country: -
US Frontline Active
1.390 million Reserve
422,000 Battle tanks
13 247 Air Force 6 612

Who has the best military in the world?
United States. The United States of America is a North American nation that is the world's most dominant economic and military power.

Which nation has the most lethal military?
States of America
The strongest military force in the world is symbolized by the star-spangled banner.

ISBN: 9798385761821
Imprint: Independently published
COPYRIGHT C EL RAMLY

Geospatial Approaches Modeling for Environmental Water Resources, land use, and Forest Sustainability

What traits distinguish an African man?

Men are defined as brave, noble, emotionally intelligent, and strong in the African culture, which is characterized by traditional ideologies and masculine ideas; as a result, they must not be irrational or emotional in the face of difficulties or overpowering circumstances (Odimegwu and Okemgbo, 2008; Van Heerden et al., 2015).

How do the guys in South Africa fare?

The gender breakdown of South Africa's total population from 2011 to 2021 is shown in this statistic. The estimated number of females in South Africa in 2021 was 30.48 million, compared to the estimated 29.56 million males living there.

ISBN: 9798385761821
Imprint: Independently published
COPYRIGHT C EL RAMLY

Geospatial Approaches Modeling for Environmental Water Resources, land use, and Forest Sustainability

How would one characterize South Africa?

South Africa is renowned for its astounding diversity, breathtaking scenery, and vibrant culture. It is one of the major hubs of African culture, a reality that has been hidden for many years by racial segregation but is now coming to light, especially in the nation's major cities.

Most South African culture is masculine.

In South Africa, women typically hold less influence than males, like gender roles in the United States.

How is dating a South African guy like?

Although South African dates are frequently straightforward, women still value chivalry, bravery, and gentlemanly behavior in men. They adore a man they can flaunt to their loved ones, after all. And the males provide without a doubt. They are typically kind and conventional, if not a tad sport obsessed.

ISBN: 9798385761821
Imprint: Independently published
COPYRIGHT C EL RAMLY

Geospatial Approaches Modeling for Environmental Water Resources, land use, and Forest Sustainability

What five qualities define a man?

Other traits often associated with men are ambition, pride, honor, competitiveness, and a spirit of adventure. These qualities don't necessarily belong to the ideal man. Instead, most guys exhibit them to differing degrees and in various ways.

Who are the inhabitants of South Africa?

Around 81% of South Africans are black, while 9% are colored, 8% are white, and 3% are Indian. After Nigeria, Ethiopia, and Egypt, the population of the nation ranks as the fourth largest in Africa and the 25th-largest in the world.

What are the prevailing gender roles in South Africa?

It is believed that a variety of ethnic groups in South Africa hold deep-rooted attitudes about gender roles, the majority of which are founded on the idea that women there are less significant or deserving of power than men. Some believe that traditional social structures in Africa are male-centric and male-dominated.

What is the reputation of South Africans?

For what is South Africa renowned? With three capitals, eleven official languages, 21 National Parks, and ten UNESCO World Heritage Sites, South Africa is known for its embrace of diversity. The nation is well-known for its breathtaking landscapes and variety of African wildlife.

What distinguishes South Africa?

At the Orange Fish Rivers Tunnel, it boasts the largest hydroelectric tunnel network in the world. The second-largest fruit exporter in the world is South Africa. Most macadamia nuts are produced in South Africa. Afrikaans is recognized as the world's newest language.

What traits distinguish Zulu men?

They are famed for their fierce fighting mentality, which has produced famous warriors throughout history, such as Shaka Zulu, who was an important figure in several Zulu wars. The Zulu tribe must be mentioned at least once in South Africa's history.

What jobs do men have in Africa?

Roles and obligations are gendered across Africa. Women are in charge of both productive and reproductive work, whereas men are predominantly in charge of productive work.

ISBN: 9798385761821
Imprint: Independently published
COPYRIGHT C EL RAMLY

Geospatial Approaches Modeling for Environmental Water Resources, land use, and Forest Sustainability

Are males from South Africa uncut?
Customs. 92% of men in North Africa and 62% of men in Sub-Saharan Africa have undergone circumcision. In contrast to the southern regions of Africa, where it is more frequently performed in newborns as a rite of passage into manhood, it is primarily conducted for religious reasons in western and northern portions of Africa.

Who arrived in South Africa first?
Australopithecus africanus is the first hominid known to have lived in southern Africa. A. robustus is believed to have first been locally documented around 2 million years ago, around the same time when Homo (? developed into Homo) displaced it.

ISBN: 9798385761821
Imprint: Independently published
COPYRIGHT C EL RAMLY

Geospatial Approaches Modeling for Environmental Water Resources, land use, and Forest Sustainability

SOUTH AFRICA CHOLORFULL CHODACHROMES PHOTOGRAPHY

ISBN: 9798385761821
Imprint: Independently published
COPYRIGHT C EL RAMLY

Geospatial Approaches Modeling for Environmental Water Resources, land use, and Forest Sustainability

ISBN: 9798385761821
Imprint: Independently published
COPYRIGHT C EL RAMLY

Geospatial Approaches Modeling for Environmental Water Resources, land use, and Forest Sustainability

ISBN: 9798385761821
Imprint: Independently published
COPYRIGHT C EL RAMLY

Geospatial Approaches Modeling for Environmental Water Resources, land use, and Forest Sustainability

ISBN: 9798385761821
Imprint: Independently published
COPYRIGHT C EL RAMLY

Geospatial Approaches Modeling for Environmental Water Resources, land use, and Forest Sustainability

Imprint: Independently published
COPYRIGHT C EL RAMLY

Geospatial Approaches Modeling for Environmental Water Resources, land use, and Forest Sustainability

ISBN: 9798385761821
Imprint: Independently published
COPYRIGHT C EL RAMLY

Geospatial Approaches Modeling for Environmental Water Resources, land use, and Forest Sustainability

ISBN: 9798385761821
Imprint: Independently published
COPYRIGHT C EL RAMLY

Geospatial Approaches Modeling for Environmental Water Resources, land use, and Forest Sustainability

ISBN: 9798385761821
Imprint: Independently published
COPYRIGHT C EL RAMLY

Geospatial Approaches Modeling for Environmental Water Resources, land use, and Forest Sustainability

ISBN: 9798385761821
Imprint: Independently published
COPYRIGHT C EL RAMLY

Geospatial Approaches Modeling for Environmental Water Resources, land use, and Forest Sustainability

ISBN: 9798385761821
Imprint: Independently published
COPYRIGHT C EL RAMLY

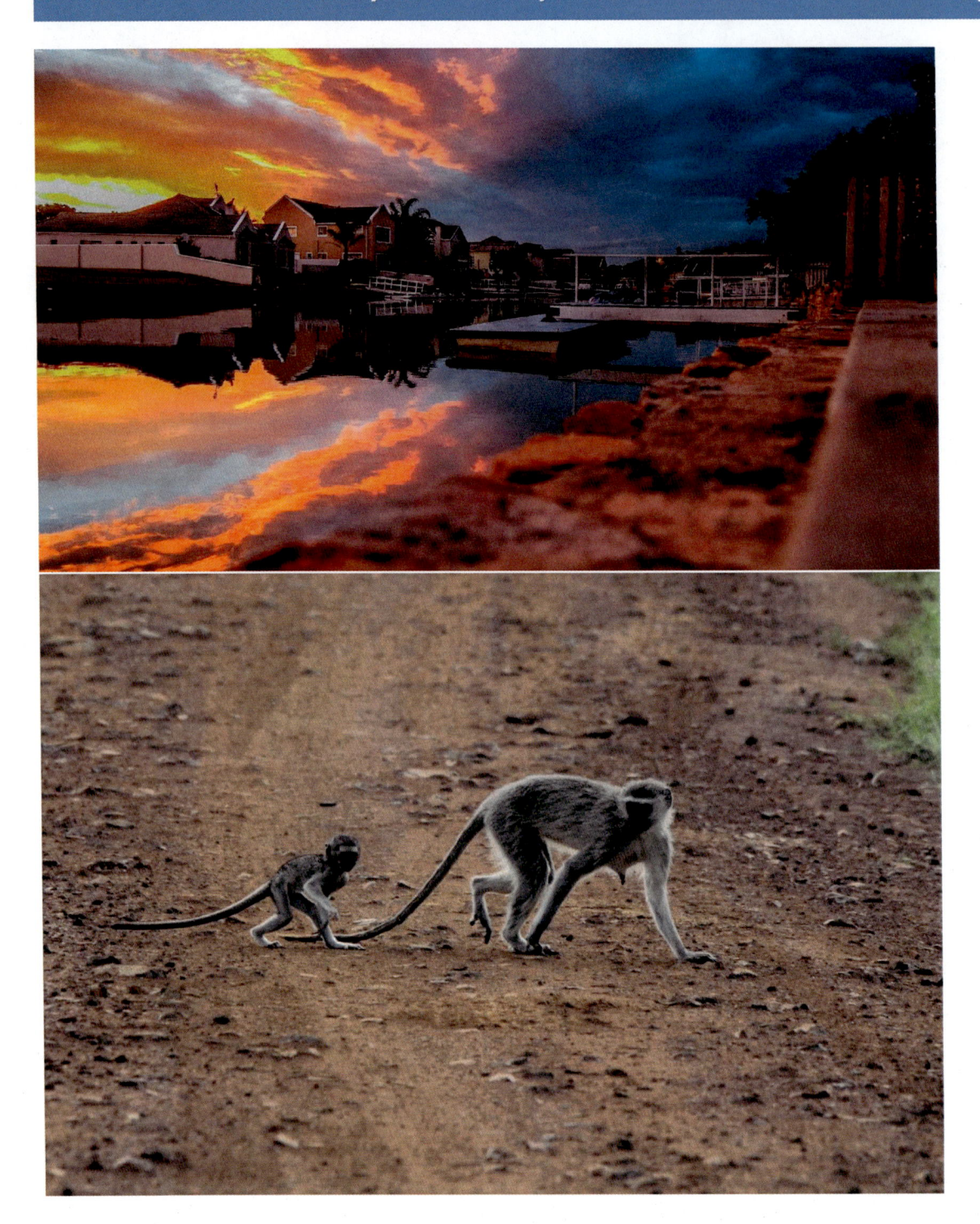

Geospatial Approaches Modeling for Environmental Water Resources, land use, and Forest Sustainability

ISBN: 9798385761821
Imprint: Independently published
COPYRIGHT C EL RAMLY

Geospatial Approaches Modeling for Environmental Water Resources, land use, and Forest Sustainability

ISBN: 9798385761821
Imprint: Independently published
COPYRIGHT C EL RAMLY

Geospatial Approaches Modeling for Environmental Water Resources, land use, and Forest Sustainability

ISBN: 9798385761821
Imprint: Independently published
COPYRIGHT C EL RAMLY

Geospatial Approaches Modeling for Environmental Water Resources, land use, and Forest Sustainability

ISBN: 9798385761821
Imprint: Independently published
COPYRIGHT C EL RAMLY

Geospatial Approaches Modeling for Environmental Water Resources, land use, and Forest Sustainability

ISBN: 9798385761821
Imprint: Independently published
COPYRIGHT C EL RAMLY

Geospatial Approaches Modeling for Environmental Water Resources, land use, and Forest Sustainability

ISBN: 9798385761821
Imprint: Independently published
COPYRIGHT C EL RAMLY

Geospatial Approaches Modeling for Environmental Water Resources, land use, and Forest Sustainability

ISBN: 9798385761821
Imprint: Independently published
COPYRIGHT C EL RAMLY

Geospatial Approaches Modeling for Environmental Water Resources, land use, and Forest Sustainability

ISBN: 9798385761821
Imprint: Independently published
COPYRIGHT C EL RAMLY

Geospatial Approaches Modeling for Environmental Water Resources, land use, and Forest Sustainability

ISBN: 9798385761821
Imprint: Independently published
COPYRIGHT C EL RAMLY

Geospatial Approaches Modeling for Environmental Water Resources, land use, and Forest Sustainability

ISBN: 9798385761821
Imprint: Independently published
COPYRIGHT C EL RAMLY

Geospatial Approaches Modeling for Environmental Water Resources, land use, and Forest Sustainability

ISBN: 9798385761821
Imprint: Independently published
COPYRIGHT C EL RAMLY

Geospatial Approaches Modeling for Environmental Water Resources, land use, and Forest Sustainability

ISBN: 9798385761821
Imprint: Independently published
COPYRIGHT C EL RAMLY

Geospatial Approaches Modeling for Environmental Water Resources, land use, and Forest Sustainability

ISBN: 9798385761821
Imprint: Independently published
COPYRIGHT C EL RAMLY

Geospatial Approaches Modeling for Environmental Water Resources, land use, and Forest Sustainability

ISBN: 9798385761821
Imprint: Independently published
COPYRIGHT C EL RAMLY

Geospatial Approaches Modeling for Environmental Water Resources, land use, and Forest Sustainability

ISBN: 9798385761821
Imprint: Independently published
COPYRIGHT C EL RAMLY

Geospatial Approaches Modeling for Environmental Water Resources, land use, and Forest Sustainability

ISBN: 9798385761821
Imprint: Independently published
COPYRIGHT C EL RAMLY

Geospatial Approaches Modeling for Environmental Water Resources, land use, and Forest Sustainability

ISBN: 9798385761821
Imprint: Independently published
COPYRIGHT C EL RAMLY

Geospatial Approaches Modeling for Environmental Water Resources, land use, and Forest Sustainability

ISBN: 9798385761821
Imprint: Independently published
COPYRIGHT C EL RAMLY

Geospatial Approaches Modeling for Environmental Water Resources, land use, and Forest Sustainability

ISBN: 9798385761821
Imprint: Independently published
COPYRIGHT C EL RAMLY

Geospatial Approaches Modeling for Environmental Water Resources, land use, and Forest Sustainability

ISBN: 9798385761821
Imprint: Independently published
COPYRIGHT C EL RAMLY

Geospatial Approaches Modeling for Environmental Water Resources, land use, and Forest Sustainability

ISBN: 9798385761821
Imprint: Independently published
COPYRIGHT C EL RAMLY

Geospatial Approaches Modeling for Environmental Water Resources, land use, and Forest Sustainability

ISBN: 9798385761821
Imprint: Independently published
COPYRIGHT C EL RAMLY

Geospatial Approaches Modeling for Environmental Water Resources, land use, and Forest Sustainability

ISBN: 9798385761821
Imprint: Independently published
COPYRIGHT C EL RAMLY

Geospatial Approaches Modeling for Environmental Water Resources, land use, and Forest Sustainability

ISBN: 9798385761821
Imprint: Independently published
COPYRIGHT C EL RAMLY

Geospatial Approaches Modeling for Environmental Water Resources, land use, and Forest Sustainability

ISBN: 9798385761821
Imprint: Independently published
COPYRIGHT C EL RAMLY

Geospatial Approaches Modeling for Environmental Water Resources, land use, and Forest Sustainability

ISBN: 9798385761821
Imprint: Independently published
COPYRIGHT C EL RAMLY

Geospatial Approaches Modeling for Environmental Water Resources, land use, and Forest Sustainability

ISBN: 9798385761821
Imprint: Independently published
COPYRIGHT C EL RAMLY

Geospatial Approaches Modeling for Environmental Water Resources, land use, and Forest Sustainability

ISBN: 9798385761821
Imprint: Independently published
COPYRIGHT C EL RAMLY

Geospatial Approaches Modeling for Environmental Water Resources, land use, and Forest Sustainability

ISBN: 9798385761821
Imprint: Independently published
COPYRIGHT C EL RAMLY

Geospatial Approaches Modeling for Environmental Water Resources, land use, and Forest Sustainability

ISBN: 9798385761821
Imprint: Independently published
COPYRIGHT C EL RAMLY

Geospatial Approaches Modeling for Environmental Water Resources, land use, and Forest Sustainability

ISBN: 9798385761821
Imprint: Independently published
COPYRIGHT C EL RAMLY

Geospatial Approaches Modeling for Environmental Water Resources, land use, and Forest Sustainability

ISBN: 9798385761821
Imprint: Independently published
COPYRIGHT C EL RAMLY

Geospatial Approaches Modeling for Environmental Water Resources, land use, and Forest Sustainability

ISBN: 9798385761821
Imprint: Independently published
COPYRIGHT C EL RAMLY

Geospatial Approaches Modeling for Environmental Water Resources, land use, and Forest Sustainability

ISBN: 9798385761821
Imprint: Independently published
COPYRIGHT C EL RAMLY

Geospatial Approaches Modeling for Environmental Water Resources, land use, and Forest Sustainability

ISBN: 9798385761821
Imprint: Independently published
COPYRIGHT C EL RAMLY

Geospatial Approaches Modeling for Environmental Water Resources, land use, and Forest Sustainability

ISBN: 9798385761821
Imprint: Independently published
COPYRIGHT C EL RAMLY

Geospatial Approaches Modeling for Environmental Water Resources, land use, and Forest Sustainability

ISBN: 9798385761821
Imprint: Independently published
COPYRIGHT C EL RAMLY

Geospatial Approaches Modeling for Environmental Water Resources, land use, and Forest Sustainability

ISBN: 9798385761821
Imprint: Independently published
COPYRIGHT C EL RAMLY

Geospatial Approaches Modeling for Environmental Water Resources, land use, and Forest Sustainability

ISBN: 9798385761821
Imprint: Independently published
COPYRIGHT C EL RAMLY

Geospatial Approaches Modeling for Environmental Water Resources, land use, and Forest Sustainability

ISBN: 9798385761821
Imprint: Independently published
COPYRIGHT C EL RAMLY

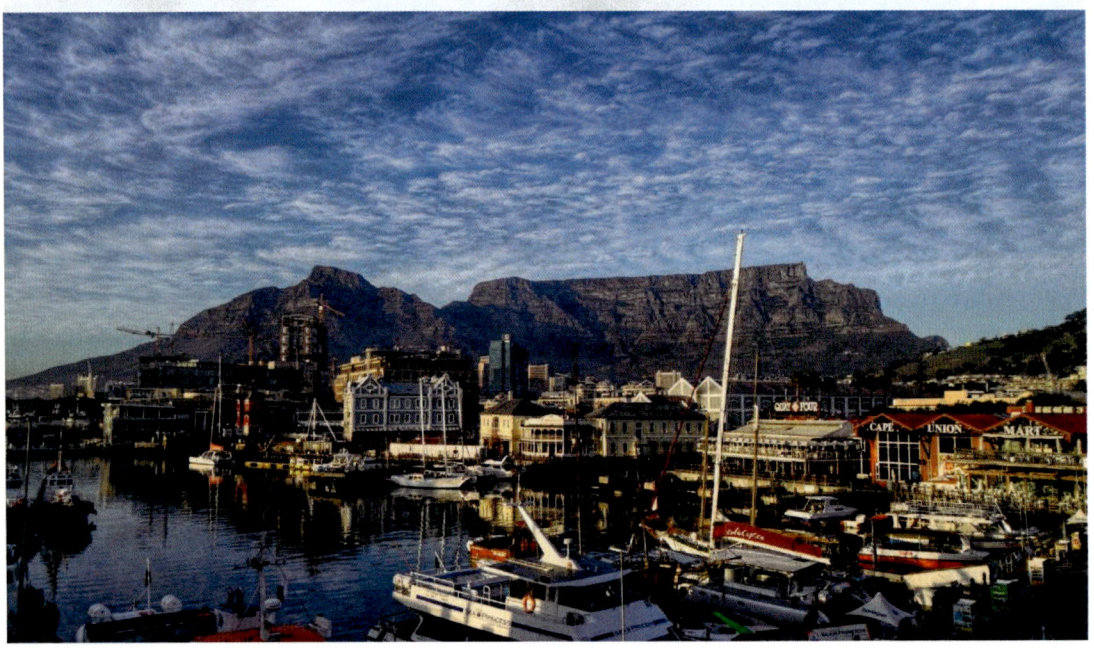

Geospatial Approaches Modeling for Environmental Water Resources, land use, and Forest Sustainability

ISBN: 9798385761821
Imprint: Independently published
COPYRIGHT C EL RAMLY

Geospatial Approaches Modeling for Environmental Water Resources, land use, and Forest Sustainability

ISBN: 9798385761821
Imprint: Independently published
COPYRIGHT C EL RAMLY

Geospatial Approaches Modeling for Environmental Water Resources, land use, and Forest Sustainability

ISBN: 9798385761821
Imprint: Independently published
COPYRIGHT C EL RAMLY

Geospatial Approaches Modeling for Environmental Water Resources, land use, and Forest Sustainability

ISBN: 9798385761821
Imprint: Independently published
COPYRIGHT C EL RAMLY

Geospatial Approaches Modeling for Environmental Water Resources, land use, and Forest Sustainability

ISBN: 9798385761821
Imprint: Independently published
COPYRIGHT C EL RAMLY

Geospatial Approaches Modeling for Environmental Water Resources, land use, and Forest Sustainability

INDEX I.
OVERVIEW OF ENVIRONMENTAL AND WATER RESOURCES
- I. WATER QUANTUM TO THE WORLD
- II. MAINTENANCE OF WATER RESOUCES
- III. GLOBAL DISTRIBUTION OF WATER RESOURCES
- IV. SEVEN PRINCIPLES OF WATER RESOURCES
- V. FOUR SORTS OF WATER RESOURCES
- VI. THE REASON WATER IS A PRECIOUS RESOURCE
- VII. THE ONE PRIMARY WATER RESOURCE
- VIII. THE NUMBER OF DIFFERENT KINDS OF WATER RESOURCES
- IX. THE BEST WATER RESOURCES
  PHOTO OF THE AUTHOR
  CONTENT

PART 1
- I. ENVIRONMENTAL AND WATER CHALLENGES FROM MANY ANGLES
- II. WATER CRISIS'S PRIMARY CAUSES
- III. WHAT IS THE TOP 5 DANGERS TO THE AVAILABILITY OF WATER?
- IV. LAND DEGRADATION REMEDIES
- V. WHAT ARE THREE WATER CHALLENGES THAT THE WORLD IS CURRENLTY FACING?
- VI. WHAT ELEMENTS HAVE AN IMPACT ON THE WATER ENVIRONMENT
- VII. WHAT POSES THE GREATEST RISK TO WATER
- VIII. WHAT CONSEQUENCES DO ENVIRONMENTAL ISSUES HAVE?
- IX. WHAT ARE THE SIX ENVIRONMENTAL FACTORS?
- X. WHAT ARE DIFFICULTIES IN MANAGING WATER?
- XI. WHAT ARE SOME FUN AQUATIC CHALLENGES?
- XII. WHAT IMPACT DOES A SCARCITY OF WATER HAVE ON THE ENVIRONMENT?
- XIII. WHAT CAUSES WATER CONTAMINATION?
  AND WHAT HARM DOES IT DO TO THE ENVIRONMENT
- XIIV. HOW DOES THE CHANGE CLIMATE AFFECT WATER LIABILITY?
- XIV. WHY IS EGYPT'S A LACK OF A PROBLEM?
- XV. WHAT ARE THE TOP THREE DANGERS TO OCEANS?

PART 1
- EARLY CIVILIZATION AQUATIC SETTING

WHY DID EARLY SOCIETIES CENTRE THEMSELVES ON WATER?
WHAT WERE THE TOP THREE REASONS WHY CIVILIZATION WERE FOUNDED CLOSE TO WATER SOURCES?
WHAT WERE THE FIRST FOUR RIVERS IN HUMAN HISTORY?
HOW WAS WATER PRESERVED IN PREHISTORIC SOCIETIES?
HOW DID EARLY SOCIETIES TRANSFER WATER?
WHY DID EARLY CIVILIZATIONS TO SETTLE CLOSE TO RIVERS?
WHY DID EARLY HUMAN DWELL NEAR BODES OF WATER?

ISBN: 9798385761821
Imprint: Independently published
COPYRIGHT C EL RAMLY

Geospatial Approaches Modeling for Environmental Water Resources, land use, and Forest Sustainability

WHAT FUNCTION DOES WATER SERVE IN A SOCIETY?
WHAT DID EARLY HUMAN DWELL NEAR BODIES OF WATER?
WHAT FUNCTION DOES WATER SERVE IN A SOCIETY?
WHAT DID ANCIENT HUMAN VALUE WATER SO HIGHLY?
WHY DO SUCCESSFUL CIVILIZATION NEED WATER SYSTEM?
WHY DID THE FIRST SOCIETIES RELY ON RIVER FLOODING?
WHAT IMPACT HAS HUMAN HAD ON WATER CIVILZATION?
WHY WERE EARLY COMMUNITIES LOCATED NEAR RIVERS?
WHY DID THE FIRST CIVILIZATION EMERGE AROUND RIVER?
WHAT EXACTLY ARE THE FOUR RIVERS CIVILIZATION?

PART II
WHAT WERE THE FOUR CIVILIZATION AND WHAT RIVERS WERE THEY LOCATED NEARBY?
WHICH RIVER VALLEY CIVILIZATION WAS THE MOST PROSPOROUS?
HOW NUMEROUS WERE THE EARLY RIVER CIVILIZATION?
DID THE PYRAMID HAVE WATER?
EGYPT USED TO BE AN OCEAN, RIGHT?
DID THE PYRAMIDS HAVE WATER?
WHAT IMPACT HAS WATER HAD ON HUMAN CIVILZATION?
WHAT WAS THE MAIN SOURCE OF WATER IN EGYPTIAN CIVILIZATION?
WHERE DID IRON AGE ACQUIRE ITS WATER?
WAS WATER PRESENT DURING THE STONE AGE?
DID THE ANCIENTS FILTER THEIR WATER?
DID IRRIGATION SYSTEMS EXIST IN ANCIENT EGYPT?
IN EGYPT, HOW IS WATER USED?
HOW DID THE ANCIENT GREEKS MOWE WATER?
HOW DOES EGYPT OBTAIN CLEAN WATER?
HOW DOES EGYPT OBTAIN CLEAN WATER?
WHERE DID ANCIENT ROME ACQUIRE ITS WATER?
WHERE DID ARABS ACQUIRE ITS WATER?
WHERE DID THE FIRST HUMANS FIND WATER?
WHERE DID ISRAEL OBTAIN ITS WATER?
WHERE DID MEDIEVAL FOLKS GET THEIR DRINKING WATER?
WAS SAUDI ARABIA EVER AN OCEAN?
WAS SAUDI ARABIA A TROPICAL RAIN FOREST?

ISBN: 9798385761821
Imprint: Independently published
COPYRIGHT C EL RAMLY

Geospatial Approaches Modeling for Environmental Water Resources, land use, and Forest Sustainability

PART III. THE WATER H$_2$O CYCLE
I. THE WATER CYCLE DEPICTS THE ON-GOING CIRCULATION OF WATER
II. THE FOUR STAGES OF WATER CYCLE
III. THE SEVEN STAGES OF THE WATER CYCLE
IV. FIVE PHASES OF WATER CYCLE
V. THE TRHREE DISTINCT STAGES OF WATER CYCLE
VI. SIGNIFICANCE OF WATER CYCLE
VII. DIFFERENCE PHASES OF WATER
VIII. WATER CYCLE REPRESENTED WITH DIAGRAM

PART IV. WATER OF HIGH QUALITY
I. THE BEST DRINKING WATER
II. THE SIGNIFICANCE OF GOOD WATER
III. TYPES OF WATER QUALITY
IV. THE BEST WATER QUALITY
V. PUREST COUNTERS WATER ARE: -
VI. SAFE WATER

PART V. SIMPLE WATER SHEDS
I. WATER SHED MEANING
II. EXCELLENCE EXAMPLE OF WATER SHED
III. BASIC COMPONENTS OF WATER SHED
IV. SIGNIFICANCE OF THE TERM WATER SHED
V. VARIOUS SORTS OF WATER SHED
VI. WHAT ARE THE FIVE MAIN WATER SHEDS?
VII. REFERENCE TO WATER SHED
VIII. ELEMENTTS THAT UP A WATER SHED
IX. GOVERANCE OF WATER SHED
X. ECONOMIC BENEFITS OF WATER SHED
XI. WHO CREATED WATER SHED?
XII. WATERS SHED IN GEOGRAPHY
XIII. WATER SHED CAUSE
XIV. DIFFERENT SORTS OF WATER RESOURCES
XV. EXACT HEALTHY WATER SHED
XVI. SIGNIFICANCE WATER SHED BIODIVERSITY
XVII. WATER SHED NATURAL OR ARTIFICIAL
XVIII. EXPLAINING WATERSHED TO A CHILD
XIX. EXACT WATER SHED RULE
XX. HOW DO WATER SHEDS EVOLVE THROUGH OUT TIME?
XXI. WHERE DOES A WATER SHED START AND WHERE DOES IT END?
XXII. CAUSATION OF WATERSHED DESTRUCTION
XXIII. WHAT IS ANOTHER WORD FOR WATER SHED?
XXIV. WHAT IS THE MOST SERIOUS THREAT TO WATER SHEDS?

ISBN: 9798385761821
Imprint: Independently published
COPYRIGHT C EL RAMLY

Geospatial Approaches Modeling for Environmental Water Resources, land use, and Forest Sustainability

XXV. WHAT EXACTLY IS A CULTURAL WATER SHED?
XXVI. EFFECT OF WATER SHED ON ECOSYSTEM
XXVII. CLIMATE CHANGE INFLUENCE ON WATER SHED
XXVIII. THE LARGEST WATER SHED IN THE WORLD

III. STREAMS AND RIVERS
- FLUMES AND RIVERS
- WHY DO RIVERS AND STREAMS EXIST?
- DISTINGUISHABLE RIVER FROM A STREAM
- TRAITS THAT RIVERS AND STREAMS HAVE
- THREE SORTS OF STRAMS EXIST
- CONNECTIVITY BETWEEN A RIVER AND STREAM
- MIGHT A RIVER BE A STREAM?
- THE SEVEN STREAMS

IV. DAMS AND RESERVOIRS IN WET LAND

- LAND SORT CONSIDERED NET
- EXAMPLE OF A DAM KIND
- IMPACT DAMS HAVE ON RIPARRIAN
- RIVER IN MOST EAST CHINA
- DAMS STRUCTURE
- WETLANDS TWO MAIN TYPES
- THREE TRAITS WET LAND HAVE
- DIFFERENCE BETWEEN A DAM
- FROM RESERVOIR
- DAM'S THREE ADVANTAGES
- PRIMARY FUNCTION OF DAMS
- THREE ISSUES DAMS HAVE

ISBN: 9798385761821
Imprint: Independently published
COPYRIGHT C EL RAMLY

Geospatial Approaches Modeling for Environmental Water Resources, land use, and Forest Sustainability

- THREE DRAW BACKS OF DAM
- WETLANDS ARE DESTROYED
- WHAT SERVES AS THE DAM PURPOSE
- DAM'S EFFECT ON THE HYDROGEN CYCLE
- DISADVANTAGES OF DAMS DRAW BACKS
- EFFECTS OF DAMS ON HUMAN LIFE
- WHY ARE DAMS USEFUL?

V. TREATMENT OF WASTEWATER AND DRINKING WATER

PRODUCTION DRKINKING WATER FROM WASTEWATER

WASTEWATER TREATMENT

WASTEWATER MIGHT BE MADE DRKINKABLE

EXIST METHODS FOR TREATING

PROCESSES IN TREATMENT OF WASTEWATER

THE SEVEN WATER TECHNIQUES

TWO PRIMARY METHODS OF TREATING WATER

FOUR FORMS OF PURIFICATION ARE EMPLOYED IN WASTEWATER

THE SEVEN WATER TECHNIQUES

TWO PRIMARY METHODS OF TREATING WATER

FOUR FORMS OF PURIFICATION ARE EMPLOYED IN WASTEWATER

KEY GOALS WATER TREATMENT

STANDARD METHODS OF WASTEWATER TREATMENT ARE THERE

DIFFERENT KINDS OF WASTEWATER TREATMENT EXIST

WATER TREATMENT IN REGRAD OF ASPECT IS CRUCIAL

ISBN: 9798385761821
Imprint: Independently published
COPYRIGHT C EL RAMLY

Geospatial Approaches Modeling for Environmental Water Resources, land use, and Forest Sustainability

OUTCOME OF THE TREATMENT OF WASTEWATER.

PART III. LAND USE

I. COMMON USES OF LAND
   a. ILLUSTRATION OF LAND USE
II. IMPORTANCE OF LAND USE
   a. SIGNIFICANCE THAT LANDS HAVE
III. TYPES OF LANDS
IV. LAND USE CATEGORY
V. FOUR FACTORS OF LAND USE
VI. ELEMENTS OF LAND USE PALNNING

PART IV

I. TOWARDS FOREST SUSTAINABILITY
- THREE ELEMENTS MAKE UP SUSTAINABLE FORESTRY
- SIGNIFICANCE THAT MAINTAING FOREST HAVE
- SUSTAINABLE FOREST MANAGEMENT
- GOAL OF SUSTAINABLE FOREST DEVELOPMENT
- SUSTAINABLE FOREST DEVELOPMENT PURSUE

II. FOREST POLICY WICKED
- IS THE LOSS FORESTS
- A WICKED PROBLEM
- DIFFICULTIES THAT ARISE
- WHEN TRYING TO MANAGE ALIVE RESOURCES A FOREST

ISBN: 9798385761821
Imprint: Independently published
COPYRIGHT C EL RAMLY

Geospatial Approaches Modeling for Environmental Water Resources, land use, and Forest Sustainability

III. MINI FOREST REVOLUTION

- TINY FORESTS EXACTLY
- MIYANAKI METHOD FOR A LITTLE FOREST REVOLUTION ENTAIL
- THE ADVANTAGES THAT TINY FOREST OFFER
- CREATION OF A MINIATURE FOREST
- ADVENTURE MIYANKI FOREST OFFER
- HOW BIG A LITTLE TREE FOREST
- ADVANTAGES OF FOREST RESTORATION
- BENEFITS OF RESTORATION

IV. MY BOOK RECOMMENDATION STORY OF THE BOOK

- PLANING FOREST MANAGEMENT
- THE TERM FOREST MANAGEMENT
- PURPOSE OF LOCAL FOREST
- SIGNIFICANCE OF MANAGING FORESTS

ISBN: 9798385761821
Imprint: Independently published
COPYRIGHT C EL RAMLY

Geospatial Approaches Modeling for Environmental Water Resources, land use, and Forest Sustainability

PART 5
PROMULGATION LAWS

I.   LAW ON WATER ALLOCATION
- WATERRESOURCE ALLOCATION AND MANAGEMENT
- STATE THAT HAS THE BEST RIGHTS
- SINGNIFICANCE OF WATER RIGHTS
- IS IT POSSIBLE TO HAVE CONSTITUTIONAL RIGHT TO WATER
- WATER RIGHTS STATED BY THE UNITED NATION
- ARTICLE 21
- WATER IS A HUMAN RIGHT OR COMMODITY
- ARTICLE "29"
- ARTICLE "31"

- LAW, INACTED BY FEDERAL STATE REGIONAL
- WHAT IS THE 1965 FEDERAL WATER QUALITY ACT?
- FEDERALAGENCIES THAT ARE CONCERNED ABOUT WATER
- CURRENT FEDERAL STATUTE
- WATER PROJECTS PLAY
- CLEAN WATER ACT OF THE CODE OF FEDERAL REVOLUTION
- ACT '2022"
- SECTION 33 OF THE WATER ACT 1974'

ISBN: 9798385761821
Imprint: Independently published
COPYRIGHT C EL RAMLY

Geospatial Approaches Modeling for Environmental Water Resources, land use, and Forest Sustainability

ISBN: 9798385761821
Imprint: Independently published
COPYRIGHT C EL RAMLY

Made in the USA
Columbia, SC
05 April 2023

5d54f435-00f4-4ac5-a61a-a3be9f26469eR01